BENEATH THE
THE
BLACK
WATER

BENEATH THE BLACK WATER

THE SEARCH FOR AN ANCIENT FISH

JON BERRY

The
History
Press

For Vic, with my love

Every effort has been made to contact the copyright holder of the quotation which appears on pp. 91–95.

First published 2011

The History Press
The Mill, Brimscombe Port
Stroud, Gloucestershire, GL5 2QG
www.thehistorypress.co.uk

British Library Cataloguing in Publication Data.
A catalogue record for this book is available from the British Library.

ISBN 978 0 7524 5837 3

Typesetting and origination by The History Press
Printed in Malta

CONTENTS

Part III: 1999–2010

ACKNOWLEDGEMENTS

I am hugely indebted, in all manner of ways, to:

Chris Yates, Simon Benham, Mathew Clayton, Abbie Wood, Jeff Barrett, Ian Spicer, Edward Barder, Simon Legg, Trevor King, Ron Greer, Mark Hassell, Teddy Morgan, Patrick Molloy, Ian Garrett, Les Darlington, Kate Davidson, Anna Jones, the Alness boys and the old man of Loch Shin. Thank you to Stephanie Turner for her picture, 'Trout'.

Above all, special thanks are owed to the clan – Mum, Dad, Vic, Chris, Edward and Ricky, who is as much my hero now as he was when we were boys.

PART I: 1997

1

THE KILDERMORIE TROUT

When we were boys, my brother Chris and I fished the loch below Kildermorie Lodge every summer. If we suspended worms beneath plastic bubble floats and cast as far as we were able, small trout would seize the bait and come cartwheeling to the shore as we wound in our lines. Cousin Ricky – our older, wiser guide on these holiday adventures – was always on hand to untangle knots or keep the midgies away with clouds of cigarette smoke. When spared these duties, he caught the most trout and usually the biggest too. The three of us fished and camped and built fires, revelling in the knowledge that our parents were 10 miles away down a slow road. It was the kind of freedom that only young boys could fully understand.

The fish we caught were magnificent and, at 10 inches or less, were perfect for the blackened frying pan that came with us. On the back of our permits, somewhere in the small print, it said that no trout of less than 12 inches was to be taken, but local size limits don't apply when you are still some distance from your teens and we were green enough to believe that trout grew no bigger.

One afternoon, as we sheltered in the boathouse from the rain, Ricky told us about the old fishing lodge further down the valley, beyond the point where the loch became the River Averon, which had a stuffed fish in the entrance hall. This giant brown trout, heavily spotted with a hooked 'kypey' jaw and black head, weighed close to 15lb and was nearer 3ft in length than 2. It was almost too spectacular to believe. Trout were small, something we held in one hand, but Ricky had been to the lodge once and had seen the monster for himself. He told us it was a ferox trout, a rare survivor from the Ice Age – primitive, predatory and almost uncatchable. When the weather relented we left the sanctuary of the boathouse and fished on, catching more small trout, but I was distracted. A bigger fish had swum into my head.

It left as suddenly as it had arrived. We were young and lived in Hampshire; giant Scottish trout – and ancient ones at that – had no legitimate place in the imagination. They may as well have been dinosaurs. Eels and perch and tench were real and could be caught from the farm ponds near home, and my brother and I pursued them with vigour. Family holidays still took us to Scotland and to Cousin Ricky, but rarely back to the old boathouse at Kildermorie. The story of the stuffed fish in the lodge was never repeated.

Inevitably, the time came when Chris and I began to stay at home and our parents drove north to Alness without us; we were teenagers now and there were other adventures to be enjoyed. Some of these involved chasing large carp in an old monastery pond. Others took place away from the water in another reality populated by girls, guitars and cars. At 16 and 17 the visceral present was everything and we found little that resonated in unlikely monster stories. Life found its momentum in the next fish, the next chord and the next Youth Club fumble. Northern Soul, crafty fags and the onerous demands of O Levels were real and could not easily be ignored. The old ferox trout and its Victorian captor were forgotten and a decade would pass before I would think of them again.

In 1997 I had to return to Scotland. My friend Martin, a London cameraman who spent much of his working life making pop videos, was with me. My own circumstances then were less glamorous; I was Head of History at an unremarkable comprehensive school, a fanatical carp angler and an unreliable boyfriend to Roo.

The road trip with Martin, above all else, was an attempt to put some space between me and an increasingly fractured relationship. Roo and I had been together for over four years and until that summer it had been special and tender, the best either of us had known. We had fished together, drunk together, grown into our twenties together. We shared a love of the same music and films, of the countryside and its wildlife, but busy lives had led us to take each other for granted and our relationship evolved into a friendship, and a sometimes distant one at that.

I was working too hard and escaping to the pond at every spare moment and our lives had marched on separately. Roo had friends whose names I barely knew; I had debts of which she was blissfully unaware. We shared a bed and an old VW Beetle, but little else of substance. Tellingly, when I had suggested that Martin and I might head north for a while, she had helped me pack and hadn't asked how long I would be gone.

Martin collected me late on a May evening, in a newly acquired but much-abused Honda saloon. It was cream with coarse tweed upholstery, high mileage and a capricious cruise control system that seemed to function entirely of its own accord. However, the stereo worked well and the road north was empty and we took turns at driving and sleeping. My partner had brought a few worries of his own and neither of us glanced in the rear-view mirror until we were well past the Scottish border. By sunrise we were pulling over for breakfast in Aviemore. Roo and work were hundreds of miles away – and so were our problems.

It felt good to be with Ricky again. Much had happened since we had last fished together; diabetes had claimed his sight and necessitated a kidney transplant. He had married and become a father and acquired a reputation as the best ghillie on the river. The skinny teenager in the boathouse had become a thick-set man with full beard and sanguine complexion, but was still unmistakably my favourite cousin. His fly-casting was as effortless as I remembered and it was only when the light fell each evening that Martin or I would need to take his arm and guide him from pool to pool. He didn't ask why I had left it so long to come back – he just led me to the fish, as he always had.

Ricky's home town of Alness – half an hour north of Inverness on the Cromarty Firth between Dingwall and Invergordon – looked like I remembered. No neon signs or architectural behemoths had sprung up in my absence. The River Averon still ran through the heart of the town and the two-room Butt and Ben cottage where my mother had been born was still at the bottom of Coul Hill; fishing tackle and permits came from Patterson's Hardware as they always had, the academy kids still got their ice-cream from Italian Tony and the highlands of Easter Ross and the Black Isle owned the horizon. Martin loved the place immediately.

Not everything in Alness was the same and to most of its people I was now a stranger. As boys, my brother and I had often been accosted by ageing spinsters as we walked down the high street. They would pinch our cheeks and squawk about us being Val Fraser's boys whilst stuffing coins in our pockets for sweets and chip suppers. Some would shuffle off recalling the handsome man in uniform who had whisked our mother away.

This no longer happened. Few locals could now remember the pretty young woman who had moved south with her twin boys and sailor husband all those years ago, and I could walk anonymously from one end of the town to the other. But it still felt like home.

On the first evening we walked down to the river as the light faded. It was late but the sun hung low in the west for an age. I had forgotten how long spring days could linger in the Highlands. We sat overlooking the Stick Pool – a deep, 50-yard hollow in the river bed in the shadow of a Victorian flood wall – listening to sea trout and a few early salmon work their way up the river. We smoked and talked and plotted the days ahead. Martin was keen to catch wild brown trout with a fly rod. I looked forward to wading in clear water and feeling the pulse of the current. I knew Ricky would put us on to a few fish and looked forward to that too.

For three full days we explored the Averon's estuary, catching small trout and salmon parr, or wandered the tributary streams taking an occasional fish from the pockets of deeper water. The trout were small and wild, heavily spotted in reds and purples. Most were released gently back into the flow, but a few were cooked and eaten by the river on an open fire, their white flesh seasoned with garlic butter and whatever wild herbs could be gathered. One morning I walked with Martin up to Bodle's Burn, the stream running past the Manse and through the graveyard where half my family were buried. It was also where I had caught my first fish – a finger-length brownie that took a worm beneath a bridge.

The fishing was simple and satisfying, and the world itself began to make a little more sense. My problems with Roo were no longer insurmountable; we needed to talk more. I needed to be more financially responsible. Perhaps I didn't need to spend quite so many weekends camped on carp pools. I could even tidy up our flat once in a while. From 500 miles away, it looked easy.

On the fourth day Ricky suggested we leave Alness and fish Loch Shin. His pal Gordy joined us and we took the Dornoch Firth road, climbing out of Easter Ross and into Sutherland. Tickets for the day were obtained from an old boy who sat chain-smoking in the loch-side hut belonging to Lairg Angling Club, and there we chose our boat from the dozen green and white wooden clinkers that were beached nearby. No other anglers were on the water that day – it was mid-week, the sky was cloudless and the water flat calm; the conditions were not at all conducive to trout fishing. The loch was beautiful though – still, fringed with hills of heather and thickets of broom, a 19-mile-long glacial scar dammed at its southernmost end but otherwise as wild as the landscape around it.

We had planned to spend our day fishing in the traditional loch style. A drogue was tied to the boat and angled to enable us to drift sideways with the current, casting our teams of wet flies ahead of us. Ricky and Gordy suggested the patterns we should use –

Bibios, Kate McClarens, Black Zulus and Pennels – and we set to our first drift with enthusiasm. Nothing moved on the surface or in the warm upper layers, and three hours later we beached, fishless and hungry, on a small island.

It was Gordy who suggested we put away our fly rods. The warm sun and absence of wind meant that the cautious trout were refusing to come up in the water to inspect our flies and, over sandwiches and freshly brewed coffee, we agreed to try spinning. The use of metal lures and treble hooks for trout would be anathema to a purist, but Martin and I were carp anglers on a road trip and had no time for dogma. Towing spinners behind a gently ticking outboard lacked the artistry of a well-presented fly, but we could probe slightly deeper in the water, perhaps catch a small brownie or two, and would be free to sleep, smoke and enjoy the sun.

I chose a black, inch-long Mepps spinner with lime green spots, for no better reason than it was the first to come to hand, and tied it on. Martin opted for a large silver spoon-shaped Toby lure. These, Gordy explained, would be dragged behind the boat on 50 yards of line, weighted by lead shot to prevent them rising in the boat's wake. We all knew that this technique – trolling – was the last resort of proper trout fishers.

Half an hour into the first troll, my outfit – a 10ft bamboo carp rod that had landed a 30-pounder the previous summer – hooped violently round, and the stillness of the afternoon was broken. Our boat was now attached by a length of taught, humming nylon to a fish that bored deep and clung to the bed of the loch. Gordy cut the engine and pulled its prop from the water. Ricky reached for the net. This was no small brown trout and for the next ten minutes we debated its identity as the creature pulled back. Could it be a pike? Too far north. A giant eel? Not a chance. A salmon? Not on such a bright day.

Eventually, the fish answered our questions for us. Quarter of an hour after it had bitten, a dark, angry trout rolled on the surface and into the net. We made for shore.

This was the first living ferox trout any of us had seen and we had no scales to weigh it. Ricky suggested somewhere between 6 and 7lb. Gordy agreed. I really couldn't say, but sat on the heather marvelling at the creature's teeth, its hooked jaw, its black head and flanks.

We fished on for an hour, but knew our allocation of miracles was used up for the day. Ricky and Gordy had heard rumours that Shin held a few ferox, but didn't know of any ever being caught. None of their pals had ever tried for them. Now, we could be certain they were there. We were astonished and joyous. Had we been wise, we might have turned our backs to the loch and walked away, but we were not.

The boat was tied up back at Lairg by four o'clock and we rushed to the tackle shop in the village to buy every spinner and lure they had. Our fly rods would remain in their canvas bags for the rest of the holiday. I didn't know it at the time, but mine would be redundant for the next few years.

I rang Roo that evening. She conceded that it was strange without me in the flat and that she missed me. We laughed a little and agreed that we hadn't done enough of that in a while. I told her about the trout and about Ricky's Kildermorie story and about how lucky we felt to have caught one of these fish. I mentioned that Martin and I would be coming back in the summer to try for another and that fishing small ponds was beginning to pale. I would need some better rods, of course, a box full of lures, a life jacket and perhaps an echo sounder. My now redundant carp-fishing equipment could go in the *Exchange and Mart* to fund future ferox hunts. It needn't cost a penny. I made promises about dusting and washing up, and showing more affection, and proclaimed the beginning of a new adventure.

I told Roo that I loved her, too, but she was too smart to fall for that.

2

THE LAST FRONTIER

By the time I returned to Wiltshire, a new coarse fishing season was about to begin. The carp had already spawned on the shallows and now skulked beneath the fronds of lily beds, awaiting the attentions of the camouflaged obsessives who chased them. The pool looked familiar, benign even. Only a year before thoughts of its aldermanic monsters had kept me awake at night and now I felt only indifference. Himalayan balsam had reclaimed its neglected banks, but I knew a path of dusty earth would encircle the pool when the fishermen returned and that the new grass would be flattened by bivouacs and their inhabitants. I wasn't keen to join them.

Pals rang to arrange night-time expeditions and plot the downfall of the very same fish we had cast for the previous summer, and the summer before that. I bought a licence, but doubted I would need it. Roo and I were still together in the nominal way of couples who share a flat and some store cards but little else, and I had assured her that I would spend less time chasing carp. She wasn't fooled, though, and claimed that I was distant, preoccupied, remote. There was something on my mind and, of course, she was right. All I could think about was Scotland and ferox trout and the wild place in which we had found them.

Ferox were different. They were unknown, and perhaps unknowable. My friends had never caught one – most had never heard of them. I championed their qualities to anybody who was willing to listen, pointing out that here was a fish that lived in a 10,000-year-old landscape, hunting silently in stygian depths. Before long, the regulars in our local pub stopped asking how the fishing was going.

I made enquiries, but nobody appeared to know how many ferox lived in Shin or the other glacial lochs of the Highlands. Was it just one? A thousand? How big did they grow? And how long did they live? I scanned every fishing book I owned for answers, and found none. In London, Martin fruitlessly asked the same questions. We spoke about giant trout every week, but they remained out of our grasp.

By contrast, my local pond held two dozen carp between 10 and 35lb in weight and had been stocked by a man named Keith. The heaviest, fattest carp in the lake was also called Keith, in his honour. Every one of us who spent each summer camped there knew these fish. Suddenly, the idea of pursuing creatures that had names and were as familiar to us as our own families seemed ridiculous. Scotland had offered a new perspective, and it became apparent that – even though there were still some carp in the pool that I had yet to catch – I had answered enough of its questions. Now, with knowledge of Sutherland and the mountains of Shin and its wild prehistoric trout, carp fishing had surrendered its hold.

Walking away from the pool was easy. I had spent much of the previous year reading the works of American fishing writers – men like Gierach, Best and McGuane – and it was their words that carried me. These were frontiersmen, wild mountain folk who camped, fished and made fires beneath the skies of America's Midwest. They fished rivers called the Roaring Fork or the Yellowstone, casting exotic flies for cutthroats and brook trout. They had no use for pet names or stocking histories. These men parked their old Ford pick-ups on dirt roads before hiking into the wilderness, and their words reeked of chewed tobacco and wood smoke. I envied them the Colorado Rockies and Montana's big sky and wished my fishing was like theirs. When ferox trout swam into view, an opportunity to disappear into the wilderness appeared with them.

I was in my mid-twenties then and would reach my mid-thirties before I realised that I had been running away. I was young and broke and all I knew was that the stark mountain landscape, the heather, the remote crofters' cottages and the deep dark waters of Shin made more sense than overdrafts or housework. They offered adventure, danger and poetry. I told Roo this and she suggested with characteristic frankness that I was being just a little bit indulgent. 'You're a history teacher, love,' she said, 'not a bloody cowboy.' I couldn't argue with her, but I couldn't stop either.

Through June and early July Martin and I continued to search for more information. We asked all our friends but most could tell us nothing. The few who did have something to tell us said much the same thing: 'get your hands on Ron Greer's book'. Greer was, it transpired, part of a cabal of scientist-fishermen operating out of Pitlochry, and his book, *Ferox Trout and Artic Charr*, summarised the findings of a group calling itself Ferox 85. We located a copy in an obscure Welsh bookshop. It led to other finds; there were occasional stories in John Bailey's books and a handful of oblique references in Victorian and Edwardian fishing guides. We hunted these down and read them all.

Some simple truths emerged. We were not the first people to have caught a ferox trout, or to have a preternatural interest in them, but we were among very few who had. Of the much-vaunted 3 million anglers in the British Isles, those who deliberately pursued *salmo ferox* could be counted in dozens, not thousands. Their collective knowledge was limited; suggested baits were dead fish or spinners that appealed to the fish's predatory instincts. The universal method was endless hours of trolling, and weeks of this could pass without incident. Many of the glacial lochs of the Highlands had small ferox populations, but not all – and where they did exist they lived quietly in the depths, in numbers that made angling for them anything but viable. Even the scientists who had tagged and tracked the fish of Lochs Rannoch and Awe had yet to ascertain whether they were an entirely unique species or an ancient cannibalistic offshoot of brown trout. Those who did chase them were fanatics, wind-blown reckless pioneers who seemed to have been absorbed into the landscape in which they hunted. Some of them were clearly a little crazy – and Martin and I wanted to join them.

There were so many unanswered questions and even if we were not the first to ask them, Martin and I knew we would, at the very least, be casting into relatively unfished waters on the periphery of British angling. The Highlands would be our big sky country, our wilderness.

Roo didn't buy into the romance or hunter-gatherer machismo of it all, but she did recognise some of the reasons why the Highlands were drawing me in. I had, she pointed out, found an excuse to go home.

This new obsession with ferox trout was not just about a fish. It was about returning to a landscape that had shaped my childhood and returning to Ricky. It was about guilt and nostalgia and turning back time to an age when life was less complicated. She knew that I hated my job, that I despised the hour-long commute to a staff room where colleagues tore each other apart, and that Scotland offered a chance to make some sense of it all. And so, she let me go.

Six weeks into the new carp season, my cousin called. His pals from the river had heard about our ferox and had been trolling on Loch Shin. The boys of Alness were now exchanging meagre wages and benefits cheques for spinners and outboard motors, and though no more had been caught, they were confident that it was only a matter of time. Martin and I were expected to join them. Ricky had been busy too; he had plundered the carcass of our first fish (which I had last seen filleted on his kitchen table) and posted a sample of scales to the research station at Pitlochry.

He had received a reply confirming that our fish had indeed been *salmo ferox* and that they would be interested to hear of any more we caught. That was reason enough for Martin and I to return; it was now a matter of scientific duty.

There was a week left of the summer term. I sold a couple of carp rods to friends at the pool, agreed an uneasy armistice with Roo and telephoned Martin to ensure that he had nothing better to do in August. An hour after the last school bell rang we were back in his cream Honda. Ahead of us was a long drive through England's industrial north, a slow road to Perth and then the interminable A9 which would take us into the Highlands. There we would find our last frontier, beneath our own big sky.

3

POLLY

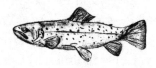

My fishing life began by the side of a Highland burn at the age of 7, with Cousin Ricky in charge and my twin brother standing next to him, waiting for his turn with the rod. Ricky was 12 or 13 and was already an expert on the rivers and streams around Alness. Within a few years he would catch record-sized salmon and sea trout from the main river, but on that spring morning our aims were more modest. Ricky wanted to show us both how to catch a small wild trout with nothing more cunning than a worm on a line. In this he was spectacularly, cataclysmically successful.

As we walked back to my grandmother's house, where Ricky lived for much of his childhood, I carried a fish between forefinger and thumb as my cousin had shown me and knew that I wanted to catch them for the rest of my life. My brother carried one of his own and had silently made a similar resolution. Ricky's work was done.

When we returned to Hampshire, we did so with a rod of our own – a 6ft solid fibre-glass model bought at Patterson's Hardware on the afternoon of that triumphant day. I still remember the price and the pleading with our mother to raise the funds. Our first rod cost £3.75 and just above the short cork handle was a decal bearing the brand and model. I thought then, and still do, that the name of the rod was more than coincidental. It was called 'The Ricky'.

Chris and I spent the next ten years fishing together, accumulating new rods and reels and falling under the spell of our neighbour's brother-in-law, who we knew as Uncle Jim. Trout were forgotten when we encountered the jewels found in southern ponds and pools: roach, tench, gudgeon and carp.

Jim was a carp fisherman and a serious one to boot; he had the matching Richard Walker glass MkIV rods, Heron bite alarms and camouflaged clothing that were compulsory among specimen hunters in the seventies, and he taught us more than we ever needed to know about how to catch fish. We were only 10 or 11 when Jim first took us to his favourite carp lake and my brother and I thought of this tall, bearded man as a god.

And so, from that first morning by a Highland burn, fishing was more than a solitary vice. I spent hundreds of days and nights besides ponds and rivers with only my thoughts for company, but the best adventures were those shared with a succession of pals. Brother Chris was always one of them, but there were others. Russ replaced Uncle Jim when the god lost his faith and started playing golf, and our gang grew to include a series of young tearaways. Adrian, Robin and Nigel the Hippy had all reached the same conclusion as my brother and I: girls were more trouble than they were worth and fishing offered a world that made sense.

The centre of that world was a chain of monastery ponds in the shadow of Titchfield Abbey in Hampshire. They were called Carron Row Farm lakes and each was no bigger than an acre. The middle pool was our favourite; it was darker, quieter and held the biggest fish. Some of its carp weighed over 10lb.

None of us could afford a season ticket, but a few hours' work around the farm in the spring was enough to earn the right to camp there for the entire summer holiday. There was no better way to recover from the trauma of O Levels, and so, in the languid heat of 1985, our gang spent eight weeks there without going home. We lived on boil-in-the-bag meals supplied by our parents and cartons of cigarettes which we sourced ourselves. The farmer offered us the use of his outhouse and its metal bath, but we rarely used either, and before long found a perverse satisfaction in our squalor. By September we were almost feral and had taken on the damp, agricultural aroma of the surroundings – but we had caught our carp.

The gang drifted apart as we grew up and each of us surrendered to a life of employment, college and romantic disasters. Some of our number appeared to forget all about the pools and their carp, but I never stopped fishing. The older I got, the more I found myself alone by the water.

This never mattered. The waters I fished in my late teens held far bigger carp and that meant there were often other fishermen around with whom I could drink tea and share stories. They were never as close to me as the old gang had been, but I was rarely truly alone. All this changed in my mid-twenties when I fell in with a loose collective of like-minded traditional anglers. I had, by then, eschewed modern fishing with its battery-powered excesses and us-and-them ruthlessness. The angling press now portrayed the fish as the enemy and the tactics of the modernists seemed increasingly militaristic. It had become excessively competitive and commercial, and after a discussion with Roo I had sold all my fancy tackle and replaced it with ancient bamboo by way of protest. The first was a battered 10ft Avon with a few inches missing from its tip, but to me it was perfect. From then on, my rods were invariably made from split-cane, my baits and tactics old-fashioned, and my fishing began to possess the magic it had when I'd winkled that trout from Ricky's burn. When I first met members of the Golden Scale Club, they welcomed me to their arcane, musty fold.

The club was infamous throughout the sport and many doubted its existence at all. Members fished simply and defiantly, embracing the values of Walton with a delightful irreverence, thumbing their noses at the bizarre spectacle that angling had become. Each member was known by a nom de plume; there was Ferneyhough and Angelus, the Pugilist and Demus, and when I livened up one of our gatherings with industrial-sized fireworks, I became Guido. There were perhaps twenty of us and no fees, badges or rules to worry about. We gathered at old inns and older waters and I soon had more fishing pals than ever before. It was then, on the banks of a carp pool, that I met Martin.

Martin wasn't a club member, but he might well have been. His tackle was old and his approach to fishing resonated perfectly with my own. Martin fished because he loved the peace found only by water and had a genuine love of the fish he sought. He was introspective, acerbic when the mood took him and we began to fish together whenever the opportunity arose.

We were both members of a carp syndicate in Hampshire. The pool was little over an acre, infested with potamogeton and lilies, and the carp were scarce but very large. Every member knew that its water was magical. Best of all, the fish had never seen cunning rigs or chemical baits and the owner was happy for us to fish there on the understanding that his carp were never subjected to modern warfare tactics. By choice and by order we fished simply with bread, worms and floats.

Martin and I caught our share each summer and began visiting the Hampshire Avon to fish for its barbel when the pool cooled in autumn and the carp slept. I introduced my friend to others in the club and before long he had earned his own nom de plume, Polly, in honour of his fondness for firing up the Kelly Kettle as we waited for bites. For the first time in over ten years I had a regular fishing pal, and even though he lived in Wimbledon, he was always willing to leave the city for quiet waters in the west.

On the final day of the river season, the club gathered on the Avon. Martin came with me and we pulled minnows and chub from the weir pool until dusk. As night fell, Ferneyhough charged down the bank demanding a camera and then a beer – he had just landed his biggest barbel, a monster of over 13lb. His prize was photographed and returned, and the club retired to the bar of the Horse and Groom to raise a toast to Isaac. It was there, during those joyous hours, that I spoke to Martin about Scotland.

Roo and I were falling apart and work was wearing me down. The overdraft had spiralled and my brother had immigrated to the Middle East with his new wife. I needed to walk away for a while and see Ricky and fish for small trout in Highland burns. I needed my friend there, too.

4

THE ROAD TO
SUTHERLAND

By sunset Martin and I were over the Scottish border. The road was quieter with every mile and as we reached the A9 the sky blackened and the landscape disappeared. Running below and beside us were some of the great salmon rivers of the Highlands and the old Far North Line to Wick, but we saw only the faint lights of the horizon and the endless barriers of the central reservation. It was a journey I knew well from childhood, one I had savoured from countless train carriages and from the back seats of dad's numerous unreliable cars, and it felt good to be making it once more. Martin and I talked of ferox, but in quiet moments I thought about Roo and home, and the classroom I had left just a few hours earlier.

Martin and I fished in a perpetual state of chaos and often arrived at a pool or river with no bait or the wrong rods, but journeys to the frontier were not to be taken so lightly; there were new rods, reels and lines among our luggage. There were life jackets too, and a mobile phone in case we became stranded. There were boxes of new lures and spinners and an inventory which we could check if we felt so inclined. But the most intriguing item of all was

Martin's little black box and, as we drove through the Grampian Mountains, he told me all about it.

The box was an echo sounder and fish finder, and Martin was evasive when I asked where it had come from. It had a 5-inch pixellated screen that promised to tell us the depth and nature of the loch bottom and to warn us if we were about to get caught in weed or grounded on a submerged island. The box would gather its data from a sensor, which we would have to attach to the hull of the boat each day using a suction cap. This sensor could spot individual fish, too, and these would also appear on our screen. There were four sizes of fishy icon, and the largest of these would only be triggered by ferox trout, pike, salmon or subaqueous dinosaurs.

The black box took us to new heights of cunning. Martin and I were traditionalists who liked to use old bamboo rods and wicker creels, so the use of a battery-powered sounder sat uneasily with us both but, if we felt guilty about our sounder, we took comfort from the fact that the Pitlochry men used them all the time. Greer mentioned them in his book, and though he advised that they could be unreliable and were no guarantee of fish, he did appear to value them and that was good enough for us.

In the weeks that followed the first capture, Martin and I had read every word of Ron Greer's book. It was technical and scientific but we knew that a grasp of ferox biology and Scottish geology would be essential if we were to catch any more. According to Greer, Shin fitted the profile of the very places that our gurus fished – ancient, glacial, impossibly big and deep. He wrote very little about our favourite loch, but did mention it briefly and that spurred us on.

The Ferox 85 group appeared more interested in the lochs further south among the hills and moors west of Pitlochry – Awe, Rannoch, Garry and Quoich. We concluded that they had yet to explore our water or discover its secrets, and so our pioneering spirit grew in the choking darkness of the Honda that night. Shin and any other lochs we stumbled upon in Sutherland would be ours alone.

As the sun rose once more we crossed the Cromarty Firth and drove the final miles into Alness. Ricky smiled broadly when we arrived. Since losing his sight my cousin had relied upon the generosity of his wife, Fran, and friends to take him to the lochs of Cromarty and Sutherland, and for this and other reasons he was glad we were there. His own collection of equipment had grown since our last visit and now included an outboard motor. He, too, had raided tackle shops for lures and spinners and had resigned himself to long days afloat. This was to be his adventure as much as it was ours.

Fran made us coffee and Ricky told us news of the Alness boys and their ferox hunt. Several of them had joined in to a greater or lesser extent, including Gordy, and others whose names I vaguely knew as the tearaways Ricky had kicked around with since his teens. Stuart, Donian, Bisto and Popper had all taken their trolling tackle to Shin since our first capture and would be joining us when work was quiet or conditions especially good.

Between them, they had fished Shin on fifteen days already, perhaps more. That amounted to over 100 hours of fishing, using at least two rods each. Martin and I were surprised that no one had caught or hooked a trout. These boys fished the river and the local lochs most days and caught wherever they went. If their nets were dry it usually meant there were no fish to be had. They, however, had been prospecting without the advantage of a little black box. We were naive enough to believe that this would make all the difference.

Four hours after arriving in Alness we left for Loch Shin. Martin and I were impossibly tired, but we wanted to see the water and cast our lines before the day was out. We drove out of Alness on the Ardross road, and passed the golf club before picking up the hill road north. Within minutes we were in the mountains, 200 metres and more above sea level, and the lush forestry of Novar had given way to stunted scrub and wilderness. To the east were the peaks of Struie and Cnoc an t-Sabhail, to the west Bien T'uinn. The road narrowed and was now lined by barber-shop posts which, Ricky told us, would show the snow plough where to go when the drifts arrived in winter. It was a reminder that we were seeing this landscape at its most benign.

After 15 miles the mountains of Easter Ross fell away and the road descended towards the Dornoch Firth. Near Adrgay we passed through a canopy of trees on a stretch of road known to locals as the Electric Hill, and Ricky instructed us to cut the engine. Here, an optical illusion told us we were going uphill, when the opposite was true. We coasted against gravity for a moment and then drove on. It was surreal, but Martin and I were exhausted and everything we saw was tinged with a lysergic strangeness.

We crossed Bonar Bridge and began to ascend once more. The quiet single street of Invershin disappeared in the rear-view mirror and then we were in Lairg. Shin extended to our left beyond the horizon, and we cheered as we saw it. The water was wide, deep and blue, and as dauntingly big as we remembered it. With more ceremony than was necessary, we pulled the magical black box from the car.

On that first day and for the next two years we were convinced that depth was the secret to catching ferox trout. The mythology of the fish, such as it was, always seemed to refer to bottomless lochs and the trout's antisocial tendencies, and so we assumed that they would be found only where ancient glaciers had created troughs and holes of 100ft or more. Our first fish had been caught in the upper layers and over relatively shallow water, but we had persuaded ourselves that this had been a fluke. Monsters always lurked in the shadows, in the underwater caverns and crevices, in places where man dare not enter – the Victorian writers said as much and so did our own logic – and so we fished as deeply as our tackle allowed. It would be a long time before we realised that we were wrong.

We knew that the men of Pitlochry used down-riggers (heavy weights on winch systems) to take their lures and baits to the depths. We didn't have that kind of equipment so peppered our lines with long strings of lead shot and trolled slowly to allow the hooks to sink behind us. When this didn't work, we began putting strips and barrels of lead on our lines to try to scour the bottom.

The fish finder proved invaluable for mapping the bottom contours. Much of Loch Shin was between 50 and 70ft deep, but there were drop-offs and shelves where the earth seemed to disappear and the numbers on our screen doubled and trebled. It was in these areas that we trolled most enthusiastically and I began to record locations in a notebook. The northern shore, on the same side as the angling club, was more promising. Here, the landscape above the waterline was steeper and this continued below the surface. The opposite shore was, for the most part, gentler and shallower. This changed further up the loch, but our attentions in that first week were focused on the first few miles of water above the boathouse.

The sounder revealed more than the bottom contours. It pinged and bleeped with every shoal of small fish and occasionally the larger icons appeared. These were invariably in the deeper water and close to the bottom and when it happened we fell silent, knowing that the ferox were beneath us. If the sounder was to be believed – and at that point we had no reason to doubt it – then our first fish had been anything but a prehistoric anomaly. There were others in Shin and all we had to do was work out how to catch them.

Each of us fished similarly, but we did try to experiment with our choice of lures. We hoped that one of us would chance upon the magic design, the one that the trout could not resist: Ricky used small plugs in yellows and greens, while Martin fished large silver spoons and I opted for lures whose colours replicated the charr and small trout that would have been the ferox's usual prey. All seemed wholly resistible to the fish.

We drove to Lairg every morning for a week. There were days when the wind prevented us going far and so we prospected the water closest to the moorings or hunkered in the car waiting for the storms to subside. On others, when Shin was calm, we trolled relentlessly from daybreak and reeled in when a full moon had risen over the loch and we could no longer see the distant glow of the lights in the angling club hut. The only breaks were for shore lunches. On these, Ricky would find shelter from the wind and discreetly inject his insulin, while Martin and I fired up our Kelly Kettles and brewed strong black coffee. Lunch was provided by Fran and was always wonderful.

By Saturday evening we were blistered from the wind and sun, exhausted from the road miles and each of us was wrestling with the prospect of failure. Above all, we were fishless.

Loch Shin was forbidden to us on a Sunday. The laws of the old churches still prevailed in the Highlands and fishing was strictly opposed by those who governed our moral well-being. All lochs and rivers were closed and the matter was not for discussion. We were broadly agnostic, but that didn't matter. The lawmakers, and perhaps the trout themselves, were not.

On our first Lord's Day we slept and cleaned our equipment and took apart the outboard motor to service its spark plugs and filters. Ricky took the opportunity to rest and to eat well, and his blood sugar levels stabilised for the first time in a week. Fran fussed over us and told us we were mad and Fly sniffed at us as we lay groaning and snoring on sofas, casting the kind of quizzical, sideways glances that only a scruffy dog can muster. The old lurcher had seen us leave every morning and return every night and perhaps wondered why we didn't smell of fish.

Martin and I walked down the river to the estuary in the afternoon, while my cousin slept. The Stick Pool was empty, so too the Sloosh and the Bridge Pool. It was only when fresh water turned to brine that we spotted fishermen – two of them in a dinghy pulling feathers through the estuary in search of mackerel. They waved, and we returned their greeting. Martin asked me why the saltier fish didn't merit Lordly protection, but I couldn't answer him.

When we got back to Ricky's I phoned Roo. She sounded well, pleased to hear from me, and asked when I would be back. I didn't know, but suspected that my money would run out within a few days. Our conversation was warm and I sensed affection in her voice, but was all too aware that we were speaking in different languages. Hers was one of realities: the electricity and telephone bills, a family divorce, the gossip from our local; mine was of mountains and dinosaur trout and the vagaries of echo sounders. It felt real enough to me, but I couldn't find words that would resonate with a girl at the other end of the country. I knew that hunting ferox in the Highlands was an indulgence I could ill afford, but I also knew that the landscape, the lochs and being with Ricky all made sense. I missed Roo, but not enough to want to go home.

Martin phoned his wife that night. Their daughter was barely walking and there were bills to pay, and it didn't surprise me when he announced that we would have to go south in a day or two. Offers of video work were hard to come by, but Martin was getting serious enquiries. It was more attention than we were getting from the trout and so we agreed to leave after one last day on the water.

Ricky was as disappointed as I was, but we promised to return later in the year. The ferox hunt was anything but over, but it couldn't override all domestic responsibility – even if we wanted it to. I didn't mention that for me it was probably too late.

Sunrise brought winds of 25mph. The boats at Shin were padlocked together and the angling club closed, and the prospect of a ferox trout on our first holiday went from slim to nothing. We sat in the cars and smoked, waiting for the storm to blow itself out, but after an hour we were sure that it would not. White caps rolled towards the dam and froth pushed up the bank below us. The old man who hired out the boats was not there, and we guessed that he knew the local weather better than us and had decided that today was not a day to go afloat. For Gordy and Ricky there was always the prospect of calmer water later in the week, but by then Martin and I would be hundreds of miles away – he filming pop stars and I making sense of life in Wiltshire.

It was time to go home, but there was somewhere even darker than the deep waters of Shin that Martin needed to visit first.

5

THE SOOTHSAYER

It was during the second visit that Ricky began to tell us stories about Sween McDonald. He lived high in the hills above the Dornoch Firth and we had passed the unmarked turning to his house every day on our journeys between Alness and Loch Shin, though Martin and I had not known. Sween McDonald was a seer, a soothsayer, and his magical forecasts were famous throughout the country. I wasn't particularly interested at first, but Martin listened carefully.

The tales seemed improbable, but four months into our ferox hunt Martin and I were already consumed by mythology and all things unlikely. We had lost a hundred hours on windswept water chasing primitive animals and could not even be certain they were there. Our entire folly was built upon rumours, half-truths and one serendipitous capture, so mystic fortune-tellers in the mountains were every bit as plausible as the fish themselves.

Everyone in Scotland's north-east corner knew about Sween McDonald. The old man was a local celebrity; he had appeared on the radio and the Scottish edition of the *Daily Mirror* had even been known to publish his annual predictions. In the more remote parts of the Highlands, such media exposure was an unassailable stamp of approval. Those who had not met him for a consultation knew someone who had. Many hundreds of Sutherland's finest had relied upon his wisdom and foresight and had thrived for doing so. For the troubled men and women of Cromarty and Sutherland, there was the doctor, the church, the lounge bar or the seer. Many chose the latter.

Approval was not universal. Alongside accounts of Sween's everyday predictions – bingo wins, kidney stones, royal deaths and marital discord – were darker tales and mischievous apocrypha. To some, the man was a practitioner of dark arts and there was a minority who would look away when he came down to Bonar Bridge for groceries. Martin and I had no such reservations and my companion was especially intrigued. Ricky had been to see Sween himself and on our second visit he encouraged us to do the same. I was unsure, but on that final day Martin's curiosity became too much for him and he pointed the Honda towards the mountains.

Silently, I wondered whether Martin ought to visit the old man. My companion was a sensitive sort, given to quiet reflection and long periods of silence. His mood could swing wildly at times and, though he was often buoyant and had an irreverent sense of humour, there were days in the boat when he would say almost nothing. We knew from Ricky's stories that Sween's consultations tended towards the apocalyptic. Should the future look bleak, he was not beyond saying so, and if Martin's forecast did not include multiple lottery wins and the imminent capture of at least one 20-pounder, it could be a long drive home.

It was early afternoon when we arrived at Sween's house. The seer lived in a rundown bungalow high above Dornoch, and geese and chickens roamed in the driveway. I had expected something stranger – gothic towers, gargoyles or a sinister greeting from a bent-backed manservant – but we were met with silence. This was fortune-telling in the Highland tradition and very different from the crystal ball con-artists of the fairgrounds.

It was Martin who was keenest to glimpse the future and so we agreed that he would see Sween first; whilst he did, I was to decide whether or not I wanted an old man's words hanging over me for eternity. Before my friend entered the house, Ricky described how the consultation would work. Sween would greet him in his study – I pictured a long oak table and chandeliers – and money would change hands. The seer would stare at him for however long it took to make an assessment and would then speak. Interruptions and flippancy were unwelcome; the seer was a serious man.

Ricky and I waited for Martin for almost an hour. I chain-smoked, unsure whether to go in when my friend returned. The present seemed odd enough and a glimpse into the future could not make it less so. Ricky, having seen the old man before, had no such decision to make. He reclined the car seat, made himself comfortable and told me his last two stories about Sween McDonald.

The first was about my cousin's own meeting with the seer ten years previously. His diabetes had become frighteningly debilitating and he was dying; his kidneys had failed, his sight had almost gone and hours every week were given over to dialysis in Inverness. With little optimism, Ricky's friends took him to Sween.

The doctors had all but given up hope for Ricky, but the local soothsayer had not. Sween reassured Ricky that he would 'make old bones' and told him to prepare for a journey to Aberdeen. The first prediction was what they had come to hear, but the second was just bizarre; Ricky had never been to Aberdeen and had no connections with the place. But, the old man had seen something.

Days later, the Alness police came looking for Ricky Fraser. They found him in a barber shop and told him there was no time to waste. A helicopter was waiting to take him south to the Granite City, where a new kidney had become available. Within hours, he underwent the transplant that would save his life.

The second story was apocryphal, but no less dramatic. There was, Ricky told me, a young man who had ridden his motorbike up to Sween's place one night to have his fortune told. The seer took his money and sat facing him across his desk, as always. Something wasn't right, however, in what Sween saw. After the shortest of pauses, the old man returned the young man's money, handed him an envelope and told him to leave. He was instructed to read its contents when he got home that night and the old man would discuss it no further.

The young man did not go home that night and never did read his letter. His bike spun off the mountain road minutes after leaving the seer and he died instantly. The envelope, when opened later, contained a single sheet of paper. Like the young man's future, it was blank.

Martin finally emerged from the house and, though there was no envelope in his hands, it was clear that he was troubled. Ricky and I agreed that it was time to leave. As I shunted the old Honda into reverse, I looked back at the seer's house and was sure I saw a gaunt grey figure behind a curtain, watching us leave. We were 5 miles down the road before Martin spoke.

'He's a very wise man, that Sween, but I don't want to talk about it. I just want to go home.'

We pressed him further but learnt no more and the subject was soon dropped. Martin and I took Ricky to Alness and left Scotland immediately. The roads were quiet and we made good time, but Martin said little during the journey. We spoke in the following weeks, about a carp lake we both knew and wanted to fish, and about the money I owed him for petrol, but not about Sween or Scotland or ferox.

By autumn the calls had stopped. I never saw Martin again.

6

TO THE WEST COAST

I arrived in Wiltshire at midnight and the flat was quiet. There were bills and letters on the dresser and evidence of Roo's presence, but no Roo. She was out with friends and it was morning before we spoke. I told her about Shin and its fish and how I planned to go back before the end of the year. We went to the pub the following evening and pretended all was well, but neither of us was convinced and within days had agreed to part. We were sad, but were smart enough to know that our lives had moved apart and in staying together we could only inhibit each other.

I packed a few bags and a bundle of rods and moved into the spare room at our friend Anna's house; Roo remained at the flat. Anna was smart and feisty with deep hazel eyes and we would soon become inseparable, but neither of us knew it then. I was just keen to avoid the ignominy of returning to my parents' house.

In late August I went back to the carp pool and caught two huge fish. The first of these was a 34-pounder, the biggest I'd caught; it took my bread flake bait unexpectedly on a hot afternoon. A year before it would have been a cause of great celebration, but ferox fishing had changed me and I greeted its capture with mild amusement. It was a beautiful creature with bronze scales and flanks the colour of butter, but it was a known fish with a name and a reputation. I took its picture and slipped it quietly back into the margins and wished it had been a trout.

Two days later I landed a 35lb carp – the one we knew as 'Keith' – with a similar lack of fanfare. I rang Roo to share the news. She was delighted for me, but she was also in Cornwall at the time with a surfboard and a new boyfriend, and couldn't talk for long. In the background I could hear laughter and I knew then that life had moved on.

A few days later Anna and I walked to our local pub. It was a quirky sort of place with a landlord whose tastes tended towards the bohemian. Quiet nights could become riotous if Al felt the 'vibe' was right. It helped if the solitary policeman in the village was there and off duty, and this was often the case. Guitars appeared from nowhere, shutters were closed, doors locked and a tiny corner of Wiltshire would descend into a hazy, Woodstock-like fug. Anna and I arrived and soon recognised that it was one of those nights. We drank ourselves into stupors, singing Beatles songs in the back room while someone played the piano.

In the early hours of the morning we realised that we ought to walk home while we still could. Anna went to bed, but I sat up to watch television and spent the next four hours following the live news feeds from Paris. There had been a car crash in an underpass, and Princess Diana was dead.

It was 31 August. A collective gloom gripped the country and soon reached epidemic proportions. I could think only about Ricky and Shin, and about the loss of Roo and Martin. The flat was gone, the Beetle too, and even the regulars in the pub could talk only about a lost princess who had meant little to them a week earlier. Al was no royalist but he knew a heavy vibe when he felt one and there would be no lock-ins or sing-alongs for a while. The autumn term was a week away and there was little else to do. On an impulse, I drove to Scotland.

Ricky and I fished for three days on Shin, trolling the south bank around the salmon cages. In Martin's absence we had no echo sounder to help us, but the Alness boys had taken a dark-flanked 5-pounder the previous week and so we knew the ferox were there. The days were flat and warm and the loch itself felt listless. We saw very few rises from feeding trout and no evidence of predators chasing them. Our rods remained stationary, so Ricky suggested that we fish elsewhere on my final day.

At dawn we crossed the Highlands to Ullapool and, with Gordy offering directions, climbed the hill roads to the north. We were on the west coast now and the temperature was cooler. A steady breeze pushed in from the Atlantic and mist hung low over every peak. The stillness of Shin was gone and we agreed that sometime during the night, summer had slipped into autumn. Eventually, two hours after leaving Alness, we arrived at Loch Veyatie.

Ricky had told me about this wild place before and had camped on its banks as a teenager, but he had never tried for the ferox trout it was rumoured to hide. Loch Shin had held our attention all year and the capture of two fish had been enough to engender a single-mindedness that took us only to Lairg. But, ever since our infant days at Kildermorie I had trusted my cousin to know where the fish would be, and if his instincts led him to the other side of the country, I was happy to follow.

Veyatie was deserted. Its 4 miles of glacial water stretched out before us and a neat green rowing boat was moored up in readiness. We carried the outboard and other equipment down to it and set up our rods. The sky was darkening and rain was in the air, and by the time we were afloat there was a relentless chop on the water. Gordy said it first and Ricky and I reluctantly agreed: there was a storm on the way and before long we would be forced back to shore.

The water was shallower than at Shin and yet darker, so we opted for small yellow and black lures that would wobble in the top layers and catch the attention of the fish. Gordy sat at the front and Ricky skippered us at the outboard, weaving along the shoreline as the rain increased. Within three hours the weather had worsened and forced us to shore, but by then we had all hooked trout. Most of those we caught were small, but two were not. They were chestnut brown, heavily spotted and weighed between 2 and 3lb. The smaller fish had been silvery, but these had large black heads and were four times the size of the little ones. They fought ferociously and had toothy predatory jaws. The three of us could reach only one conclusion: these were young ferox.

We crossed the Highlands in joyous mood. It seemed that we had found a loch where the smaller ferox were catchable, though we couldn't be certain of this without sending scales to the boffins of Pitlochry. If juvenile fish were present in Veyatie, it was not unreasonable to expect there to be older specimens of great size living in the depths. All we had to do was find a way to catch them. Loch Shin was closer and bigger and would remain our first love, but we would simply have to return to the darker waters of the west.

The Alness boys saw out the season on Loch Shin, but no more ferox came to their boats. We urged them all to go back to Ullapool, but none went – it was too far and too expensive, they said, and they were right. Our visit had been organised by Ricky, who knew the bailiff well enough to arrange it without money changing hands, but more usually the ticket for a day on Veyatie cost half a week's Giro and that was beyond the boys from the village. It was beyond me too, but I had a winter ahead of me to raise some money. We began hatching plans to return in the spring.

PART II: 1998

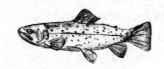

7

THE REVEREND'S TROUT

The autumn term began, but when I should have been thinking about marking books or making money, I usually daydreamed about giant trout. My fold-out map of the Highlands became a mess of scribbles and circles as every possible ferox loch was identified. All significant patches of blue were noted, and their glacial credentials questioned. If they were big and deep they were short-listed, and cross-referenced against a growing collection of pre-war *Where to Fish* guidebooks. I had newer editions, but these seemed preoccupied with man-made put-and-take rainbow trout fisheries and we felt that it was the older publications that would list *salmo ferox*'s presence. The fish, after all, belonged to an older landscape and a forgotten angling past. In truth, the guides rarely mentioned ferox by name, but some alluded to monsters that were reluctant to rise to a fly – and that was enough to go on.

Each of these finds was discussed at length with Ricky, who was charged with investigating how we might get permission to fish them. Meanwhile, Gordy and the rest of the Alness boys went pike fishing around the lochs of Sutherland and Easter Ross, always alert for signs or rumours of ferox.

Throughout the winter, Ricky and I made plans for spring and summer. Long days on Loch Shin were a certainty, but our list of potential waters grew. The west coast had shown great promise, but as memories of the summer faded, we began to wonder whether the Veyatie fish had been ferox at all, or simply larger-than-average brownies. There was no way to be sure; we had returned them to the loch and so the opportunity to take scale samples was lost. To confuse us further, the scientists themselves seemed undecided whether ferox were a distinct strain of trout at all, or simply brown trout that had out-lived and out-grown their smaller companions. Trout of 2 and 3lb, particularly those that fed on other fish and had taken on the darker, angry demeanour of true ferox, might just be especially large wild brown trout. We agreed – in the interests of simplicity and with absolutely no scientific rigour – to regard fish above 4lb as ferox trout. Two and three-pounders would be classified as 'maybes' and it was only in the following years that we would find out that we had made yet another mistake.

This figure wasn't reached in an entirely arbitrary fashion. None of us had ever heard of a fly-feeding brownie of that size coming from the Highland lochs we fished. Shin and Kildermorie and the other places we knew were not rich waters. In each, the trout stayed small on a diet of flies and insects and rarely topped a pound in weight. Most were half that size, and so it seemed reasonable to agree that 4-pounders were a different creature altogether, even if the Pitlochry men couldn't prove it. And yet, every time I looked at the transparencies we had taken on the Veyatie shoreline, the fish looked more and more like the dark and predatory animals we imagined.

The winter passed slowly, with occasional calls from Ricky when he had news of a big pike for one of the boys or whispers of possible ferox lochs. I had moved into the main bedroom at Anna's and so her spare room was now given over to bamboo and tackle boxes and a wall chart of the Highlands. I had a new job, albeit a part-time and unpaid one, working in a traditional tackle shop in Stow-on-the-Wold. The owner, Simon, was a good friend and fellow cane rod enthusiast and was happy for me to be rewarded in stock. In this way, over the cold months, I amassed a formidable collection of American and Swedish lures and took home two split-cane Hardy LRH spinning rods. These 1950s' models were just over 9ft in length and would allow me to chase ferox with a little more panache. In addition, Simon lent me his glass-fibre Hardy carp rods, which offered greater length and a softer action. He didn't know it then, but he wouldn't see them again for many years.

Simon's shop also stocked angling books, old and new. When the days were quiet, and they often were, we would sit and read. This was a time when chain-smoking in tackle shops was positively encouraged and we did this too, reclining in old chairs and only removing our feet from the leather-topped bankers' desk when a customer arrived. Sometimes this didn't happen at all and we would leave a note on the door and decamp to the Talbot Hotel for a pint, or simply read until it was time to close up. Inevitably, the time came when Simon acknowledged that demand for split-cane rods was not what he had hoped it might be and that his traditional tackle shop could not survive in an age of online bar-gains and mass-produced carbon equipment – but for that winter, at least, we enjoyed ourselves.

For much of the time, possibly too much, I talked to Simon about ferox trout. His loves – alongside a gorgeous but unreliable girlfriend – were tench ponds and wild carp, and he thought it daft that his impoverished Saturday boy was forever stocking up on lures for jaunts to the other end of the British Isles. That said, his knowledge of old angling literature was impressive and he was able to direct me towards numerous forgotten tomes that made refer-ence to my favourite fish. The ferox library grew and with it the list of lochs to investigate.

These old books suggested little in terms of techniques; their authors were ostensibly salmon and trout men who would pay a ghillie to row them up and down a loch when the river was out of sorts. They were almost always spinning with minnows or lures for whatever came along, and their accounts usually ended with a lost fish, a cursing ghillie at the oars and the sport himself standing helplessly with limp rod and a broken silk line flapping in the breeze.

I loved these stories. They added to the mystique that we had already bestowed upon the fish and offered hope that they could at least be hooked. The tales, even allowing for a little Victorian exaggeration, were wild and windswept and heroic. The authors wrote evocatively of a Highland landscape I recognised. The mountains and waters they described had changed little in a century, but I knew that the twentieth century's worst excesses were just beginning to reach Scotland's remotest corners. Salmon cages were now floating on Shin, threatening the ecology of a fragile wilderness, and a wind farm had recently been built on the hills overlooking Loch Kildermorie. There was no telling what else might happen and so I resolved to spend as much time as possible in Scotland; if progress was marching inexorably towards our final frontier, time was of the essence.

As winter came to an end, three more old books came my way. These were not from Simon's shop, but turned up in an antique shop in Ludgershall, the small barrack town I passed through on the way to work. I stopped there for a break and a chat whenever I could, but this was rare – its owner kept even more idiosyncratic hours than Simon and the place was usually closed. I liked it immensely; it was not a conventional antique shop of the middle-class market town variety, more a bizarre roadside emporium in which one might find anything from Napoleonic battledress to a stuffed crocodile. Occasionally, bundles of greenheart rods would be found in a dark corner. Brass reels, gaffs and eel forks were not unknown, and though the shop never seemed to have any customers, it appeared that the stock changed entirely between each of my visits. I rarely bought anything there, but always left with the proprietor's promise ringing in my ears: 'if anything fishy turns up, I'll put it aside for you.'

One March evening I walked in to find a pile of angling books waiting for me. There were several of no interest: sea-fishing manuals, boys' instructional books and even guides to competitive match fishing on canals. Three, however, were older and much more intriguing. Each had lost its dust jacket and carried the musty smell of old pages and ancient words. They were within my budget and I rushed home to Anna's to read them.

The first made no mention of ferox, or the ordinary trouts. It was written by E.G. Boulenger and was called *Queer Fish*. The author was once director of the Zoological Society's aquarium, and wrote of flying fish, nesting fish, sea-dwelling oddities and strange aquatic mammals. It was a 1925 edition and contained a delightful pencil-led inscription: '*a gift from mother for being Top Boy in form Upper 1B in Taunton's School*'. I couldn't help but wonder whether its owner, R. Lee of Itchen, was once as obsessed with rare fish as I.

The second was a 1925 edition of John Watson's *Lake District Fisheries*. In the chapter on Lake Windermere, Watson wrote of the huge charr population and the popularity of trolling for trout, hinting of fish between 5 and 8lb and claiming '*all my biggest trout are got in this way*'. Anna was impressed by this and so was I; we could now add a possible English venue to our ferox trout hunt and she could indulge her love of dinghy sailing at the same time.

It was the third book which proved to be the biggest prize. R. Macdonald Robertson's *Wade the River, Drift the Loch* was a fabulous collection of fishing stories from the Highlands and was first published in the 1940s. The author wrote of waters I knew and had fished, of ancient ghillies, of ghosts on the moors and mermaids swimming at Cape Wrath. He described, too, the popular methods of the day, particularly worm and fly fishing, but also trolling. But, it was the photograph on page 100 which had me leaping for joy. On that yellowing page, an old man in trilby and dog collar stared into the camera with a look of wonder. In his arms was a cast of his greatest catch – a giant Veyatie ferox trout.

The captor, the Reverend Walter E. Lee of Edinburgh, was a friend of Robertson's in the days when he had ministered to the good people of Perth. The two of them had long speculated about the identity of an infamous water monster that was reputed to live beneath the Black Falls of Veyatie and, in July 1938, the man of

God had answered their questions by catching it. When he did, he gave the story to his pal for his book:

It had been wet weather during my stay at Altnacealdach, and when I reached Loch Veyatie I found there was a fairly stiff westerly breeze blowing in my face up the water, so I decided to row in the teeth of the wind and get some drifts back to the anchorage. My boatman suggested that as it would be a stiff pull, I should have a try with the minnow, therefore I went to the burn which feeds the loch and caught a couple of small trout, one of which I affixed to an Archer Spinner which I trolled behind the boat. We had not rowed many hundreds of yards when there was a strong pull and the splutter of a big trout, but I never dreamt of so large a fish as it turned out to be. My small net was useless and I did not think of running the boat aground to grass the monster, as I should have done. We hauled it aboard by the gills at the second attempt. It was easy to imagine my surprise and delight when he turned the scales at 16lbs. I believe there is no record of a larger trout being caught on Veyatie than this one. He measured nearly a yard in length and was about half as much in girth. A cast of this fish now adorns the lounge of the Hotel at Altnacealdach.

It would have been easy to disregard a 60-year-old monster story, but I knew that the hills and waters above Ullapool had changed little in that time. Veyatie was as wild as it had been when the Reverend and his ghillie had set out that day – and so whatever chemistry or magic existed in the loch and had conjured up their monster was likely to still be there. I spoke to Ricky, and the story of the Reverend's trout was passed to the boys of Alness. Our plans for Shin and Kildermorie would remain unchanged, but later in the year we would drive into the hills of the west and gather beneath the Black Falls to see if we couldn't catch a monster of our own.

8

PREDATOR AND PREY

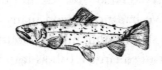

Slowly, we began to understand a little more about our quarry – not through captures, of which there had been very few, but through reading, researching and bothering the men of Pitlochry. Ricky had contacted the scientists over the winter and had been directed towards obscure scientific papers in publications like *The Journal of Fish Biology*. It was reassuring to know that somewhere out there, good and wise men had devoted their working lives to developing a scholarly body of knowledge of these fish and protecting their environment.

It had been so much easier when I had been a simple, happy carp fisher. Everyone knew that carp had come across from Eastern Europe in the Middle Ages to satisfy the hunger of monks, and that they were now bred, less prosaically, in fish farms in Surrey and Hampshire. Their existence had never depended upon the fortunes of a fragile ecosystem. Famously, carp could survive for decades in the muddiest of puddles. When my brother and I were younger we had been told, by a proper camouflaged carp fanatic, that a 20-pounder could live out of water for twenty-four hours if it had to. 'It's true,' he had said, 'but they don't bloody like it.' So we caught them, weighed them and returned them in the hope that they would be even bigger when they next fell for our traps. If the fish themselves got old or tired or tatty from recaptures, they could be removed and replaced. The entire, slightly ludicrous process was man-made. It required as much empathy with the natural world as a round of crazy golf.

Understanding the place of ferox trout in the grand scheme was entirely different. Greer and the older writers helped us and, though there was much in the scientific papers that was difficult to comprehend, we began to piece the story together.

We knew that the presence of ferox trout in the Highlands of Scotland, and to a lesser extent in the larger waters of the Lake District, Wales and Ireland, could be attributed to the advances and retreats of the great glaciers during the last Ice Age. Ferox trout belonged to a landscape that was once home to reindeer, bears and mammoths. They were with us only because the Ice Age lingered on below the surface, offering stability and protection while the land around adapted to a new era. Man's advance northwards and the urbanisation of much of the landscape had done great harm to most of the post-glacial fauna, but the ferox – alongside ptarmigan and charr – had survived it all. They were reminders of a climatic event that was all but forgotten.

We knew, too, that the genetic identity of ferox was not entirely secure. They belonged to the family *Salmonidae*, which encompasses trout, charr and salmon. Classification within this family has long been muddled, not least because much of the work done by biologists pre-dated the development of DNA techniques.

The propensity of trout to diversify into localised sub-species did much to contradict the efforts of early scientists like Houghton and Berkenhout, and did little to help us either. We knew that there were many varieties of brown trout, some found in only one or two waters, as well as different races of ferox, sometimes existing in colonies within the same loch. Whether these were each unique or merely subtle variations within one sub-species depended upon who we asked. We also understood that, ultimately, ferox were just giant brown trout; their separation from the other trout in any water might be attributed to genetics, circumstance or caprice. The scientists, on this point, seemed unsure. We were in no position to contribute to the debate – we couldn't catch any of them.

Ricky and I understood this much, but no more. We just knew that these huge fish, which predated on charr and smaller trout on the waters we fished but were known to snatch lemmings from the surface of waters in Norway, differed from anything else available to the British angler. Their existence was a miraculous story of resilience – against climatic change, against other predators, against nature's lack of sentiment and against man's talent for buggering up the environment for his own ends. For reasons scientific and otherwise, they left us in awe.

Another part of the attraction of ferox trout to our small group was the evocative name given to them. The effect was subconscious but very real. In 1789 John Berkenhout had written of the great lake trout of Europe, describing fish 'in the north' that reached weights of 50lb and attaching the Latin moniker *salmo lacustris* to them. His efforts at classification, however worthy, did not last. Fifty years later, angler Sir William Jardine coined the bluntly evocative term 'ferox' and this stuck. It had a diabolical resonance that was hard to ignore.

With this name, then, came a pejorative reputation. Jardine's choice of words implied ferociousness, even cannibalism, and divided the Victorian angling public into a tiny minority who sought them out and a majority who disliked them. It was unfair and anthropomorphic, and ignored the reality that almost all species of fish ate their young or plundered the unhatched eggs of their kind. But, it was ferox that were labelled, and the literature of the day helped cement this reputation. The best-known example of this misplaced ferox-phobia was found in Robert Browning's *The Inn Album* of 1875. The poem, structured around the messages sent between two couples in a visitor's book, was published widely and to popular acclaim. Among its 3,500 lines, Browning included the following:

Grim o'er the mirror on the mantelpiece,
Varnished and coffined, salmo ferox glares.

If the predator had us confused, the prey was no less baffling. The boffins and the old writers were unanimous on one thing: to understand the quarry, it was necessary to understand the fish it ate too. It seemed simple enough: ferox ate charr, charr lived in deep lochs, charr were silver with hints of blues and purples, and this would guide our choice of lures. What else did we need to know? If we wanted to catch ferox, and we certainly did, we ought to offer them something akin to their natural diet. That meant charr or something close enough to the real thing as to make no difference.

We decided, on the basis that they were perilously rare and notoriously difficult to obtain, that we would not use charr for bait. It seemed wasteful and unnecessary. We would fish with lures, in colours and sizes that might remind the trout of the charr they really sought.

But, this was ferox fishing, and we already knew that nothing was as simple as it first seemed. The ferox I had caught had taken a small black spinner with green spots. The Alness boys' singular triumph had been to a silver, spoon-shaped lure trolled alongside the salmon cages. The Veyatie trout, which had quite possibly been ferox and had certainly taken our lures in the belief that they were fish, had fallen for small plugs in shades of lime green and yellow. None of our few successes had been to charr-like baits, even though we had used them extensively. Then there were the questions of shape and depth.

These questions were harder to answer than in other forms of angling. The fly fisherman could base his selections on an examination of what was happening on the water's surface at a given time; if olive mayflies were hatching, he could rummage in his fly tin for something approximate and reasonably hope to catch. Carp anglers also knew where and how their fish fed – grazing on the surface or troughing among the bottom silt – and similarly could rely upon visual clues. We were trolling deep water, however, and any indication of ferox feeding habits would come only after a capture. Somehow we had to remove our dependence on serendipity and that meant understanding how ferox fed.

The scientists had already done much work on this. If the existence of a lab-coated subculture of ferox tyros had surprised us, the discovery that there was an even bigger scientific community dedicated to the study of arctic charr impressed us even more. These were single-minded addicts who thought nothing of donning wetsuits and diving into arctic waters to verify the most obscure academic hunches. They wrote at length of the subtle differences between bottom-dwelling benthic and open-water pelagic charr within the same lake, and attended conferences where they argued vociferously – but with scholarly decency, of course – about charr feeding habits. We discovered the existence of these devotees in the same obscure journals that had published ferox papers, and we heartily approved.

The most significant group appeared to be the International Society of Arctic Charr Fanatics, but there were other individuals and groups, and some overlap with the scientists at Pitlochry. All of them knew more about charr than we felt the need to know, or had the ability to comprehend. We were simple fishermen, and it began to feel like we had stumbled upon the activities of a secret society.

If we didn't understand some of the theories espoused by the scientists, we at least understood the reasons for their fanaticism. Charr were just beautiful. They were enigmatic, too, with an ability to adapt to hostile environments and develop as many regional variations as the trout that ate them. Some were bottom-dwellers, others fed in mid-water, while others still were known to sup flies from the surface layers. A few had been known to disappear to the bottom and 'go ferox' themselves. We knew that the ferox we sought ate charr, but found ourselves asking the question: what kind of charr are they eating?

All of this fascinated us, but didn't help us in our efforts to catch something. Ricky and I could only conclude that ferox ate charr at whatever depth they found them, but were also partial to trout, whitefish, coarse fish and hapless rodents. We would continue to pester the scientists and read their publications, but most of all we would just keep fishing.

What had become clearer was that both the ferox and their prey were participants in a much wider and precariously balanced habitat. Both were indicators of the health of the sub-arctic Highlands and deserved better than they were getting from their human neighbours. Commercial fish farms, non-indigenous species introductions, pollution and increasing urbanisation all threatened the presence of the fish we sought. The landscape in which we sought them was beautiful and remarkable, but it was far from secure. As our second season approached we were still on a monster hunt, but it risked becoming an environmental crusade. And in all this, we were eternally grateful for the hard science provided by the men of Pitlochry, even if we barely understood a word of it.

9

AMONG THE BLACK STUFF

As Easter approached, Ricky called. My cousin was concerned about high winds in Sutherland and the Met Office's view that these would continue for at least two more weeks. They had rain as well, the relentless sleety kind, and he wondered whether we ought to postpone the next visit. Loch Shin would be perilous and unpleasant and we might drive there only to be forced off the water before we had even started.

With Shin in angry mood, we talked of other places where our search might continue. We could take our chances on the lochs further south, the very ones where the scientists caught their monsters, and hope that the weather was calmer there than in Sutherland. I was keen to try them, not least because it was in Awe and Rannoch where the 20-pounders were known to live, but it would necessitate roughing it by the loch and sourcing our own boat, and my older and wiser cousin overruled me. He cited costs as prohibitive, but the matter was more complicated than that. Ricky's health was rarely discussed, but we both knew that a week in a wet tent would wreak havoc with his blood sugar levels.

I remembered Watson's book and the big trout of Windermere, and suggested to Anna that we all decamp to the Lake District for a week, but this was fraught with problems. We would be arriving at the start of the holiday season, when boats were hired by the hour and hotels were full. The tourist industry in the northwest was not constructed around the needs of ferox anglers who wanted boats from dawn to dusk, and if we managed to get afloat we would be trolling among paddle steamers, windsurfers and jet skiers. Ricky was blind and I was inexperienced and with either of us at the helm it could be calamitous. With a week to go before the end of term, Anna suggested Ireland.

Anna was a doctor and a sailor and formidably bright, but her greatest asset was her energy for all things new. Throughout the winter she had listened patiently to the ongoing ferox dialogue and had soon begun to participate. Now she wanted to catch one.

The west coast of Ireland was wild and romantic and that was where Anna wanted to go, but her plans came with a compromise. It would be a holiday, and fishing would form part of it but not all. She and I could explore castles and eat in white stone pubs and do the things that young couples should do. Ricky could fish every day and we would join him for some of them, and we might just land a wonderful, monstrous trout. I considered negotiating, but was smart enough to say nothing. It was Anna's money and car that would take us there, after all.

Ricky thought it an excellent plan – there was no expectation that he be dragged around castles – and we hastily discussed possible locations. We knew that ferox had been caught in the Galway loughs, Corrib and Mask, and that similar giants lived in Lough Melvin in County Fermanagh, hunting the indigenous sonaghan and gillaroo trout. All three had history and fitted the topographical profiles, and there were boatmen on each who could row us to known spots, but we preferred the prospect of trolling somewhere with more secrets. Our Scottish endeavours had been on lochs with the vaguest of reputations and it seemed right that we should abandon the beaten track in Ireland, too. The final choice belonged to Anna.

On a Friday in April, Ricky flew from Inverness to London and Anna collected him while I worked. At midnight we boarded the car ferry at Fishguard and by lunchtime the following day we were standing on the shore at Dromineer Bay on the banks of Lough Derg in Tipperary. Anna had rented us a cottage on its banks, less than a hundred yards from a pub. Nights in the Whiskey Still beckoned; so too did a week in which we could explore the 32,000 acres of deep glacial waters outside our front door.

Our first Irish night could only be spent in the pub. The crossing had been long and turbulent, the drive across the island similarly traumatic, and we succumbed to the instinct that surfaces in all new arrivals – a riotous evening among the black stuff. The Whiskey Still offered this and chasers of Tullamore Dew, and by midnight we had given in to every temptation. There was singing, a brief and oddly good-natured fight between two local boys and assurances from the regulars that we had landed at a lough full of fish. Frank the Landlord took us aside in the early hours and told us there was only one man we should talk to if we hoped to catch a trout. His name was Teddy Morgan.

Night became morning and Frank finally threw us out, but not before Teddy had become our new best friend. We learnt that he was the wise old sage of Derg, the finest boatman on the lough with a luxurious clinker for hire and a preternatural knowledge of where we should cast our lines. We were also told that fishing for the big trout was futile before the dapping season arrived in May and that no one bothered trolling for them, but he was willing to take us out to try nonetheless – and for only 50 punts a day. More of Anna's money was handed over and Teddy became ours for the week; he would meet us on the quay by the pub on Monday morning. We asked if we could fish on Sunday, which had already begun, but our wise ghillie knew that the black stuff and the dew had seized us. Besides, Mass began in four hours. These were papal lands and waters and even mythical trout needed a day of rest.

We rose later in the day and explored the lough by car. We stopped to investigate the shore at Ryan's Point and Garrykennedy, marvelling at the dozens of small islands and the white caps crashing over them. Later, we drove up to the Arra Mountains to find the Graves of the Leinstermen, stopping at a small hill pool whose surface was dotted with the concentric ripples of rising trout. Descending towards the lough's end, we saw the remains of ancient slate quarries hidden among slopes of bog heather. Ricky and I could now discard the scepticism of our new friends at the Whiskey Still; the presence of ferox was in no doubt. The topography was right, the lough ran long and deep, but more importantly we were in a land where magic and truth fused into one.

Sunday evening was fair but a biting south-westerly was still blowing up from Limerick. Over supper and a pint in Gooser's Bar at Killaloe, we wondered if Teddy's boat was strong enough and whether its captain would set out on an angry lough. Anna quietly reminded us that there were other things to see and do.

By dawn the waves outside our door had become ripples. Teddy met us by the quay, carrying an armful of life jackets. There were several clinkers and dinghies tied up, but Teddy's was unquestionably the most impressive – 19ft long, fully appointed with chairs and rod holders, lovingly painted in a dark celtic green and bursting with tackle boxes. Ricky took the bow, me the middle thwart and Anna sat with Teddy at the stern.

The old sage took us straight to the far side of the lough opposite Youghal Bay as we strung line through our rods and rummaged for inspiration in our lure boxes. Ricky and I fancied rattling divers, but Teddy had other ideas and insisted we both start with a local favourite – the Lane Minnow. These, he told us, had been handmade and painted in County Limerick for almost fifty years; they were the killing pattern for pike and wild trout throughout the Shannon system. Those he thrust in our hands were scratched and chewed from previous encounters – with pike, we guessed – and Ricky and I tied them on.

The first day passed quickly and Teddy's stories filled the hours. He told of us of the wife he'd lost to a brain haemorrhage and how the lough had become the second love of his life. There were tales of enormous pike caught and lost, and gossip about the strange Germans who had set up camp on one of Derg's islands years ago, and who had made it their permanent home. We were told again that May was the only time the big brown trout would rise to anglers' baits, supping their imitation mayflies dangled on long dapping rods. 'Come back in a month,' we were told. 'You'll get your monster then.'

Anna was enthralled by the man and by the 10lb pike she caught. Ricky and I caught pike, too, though ours were smaller. The trout, of course, were nowhere to be seen. Teddy was evasive on the subject and conjured up a new tale whenever we asked about them; by supper time, when our trolling ended for the day, he had Ricky and I convinced that we were casting for rumours.

Frank met us as we pulled in by the pub and offered us a consolation drink, but Teddy's stories weren't over for the day. 'Come and see something now, you three,' he said, when the boat was secured, and so we followed him on foot to a bungalow close to the shore. In a tidy front room, perched above the television, was a glass case with a stuffed fish in it.

'Is that what you're after?' asked the sage. Ricky and I didn't need to reply. The fish was a Lough Derg ferox, a little over 10lb in weight with ink black spots and a primitive, beautiful demeanour which we'd encountered all too infrequently on Shin and Veyatie. Gold script on the case told us the identity of the captor: *T. Morgan of Dromineer*. The sage laughed and suggested that he buy the first round.

That night the winds returned. The lough swelled and the white caps rolled over the islands. For three days we were land-bound and Anna got to visit the castles we'd talked about and do the other things I had promised. Ricky and I stood at the door each morning wondering how many more fish like Teddy's swam out there, somewhere, in front of us. It would be Friday before he took us on the water again.

When Teddy met us at the quay on our final morning, he agreed with our forecasts; the wind had dropped sufficiently and we could go fishing. A steady south-westerly remained and carried light rain with it, but the lough was calmer than it had been all week and the wise man of Derg was sure his boat could handle it. Throughout the week the lough had coloured up as earth-stained groundwater had dripped in from the fields and feeder streams, and Ricky and I knew this made the prospects of a ferox trout slighter than ever. Three fishless days of castles and slate mines had taken its toll – we just needed to cast our lines.

There were to be no life jackets that day. It was Good Friday, a holy day but not a holiday across the Republic, and half the country had shut down in observance. That included the quayside office where Teddy stowed his gear and so we would have to take to the water as St Peter intended, with only our nets and good intentions. Anna asked whether we were permitted on the lough without flotation devices and how this might jeopardise Teddy's licence, but the captain just muttered about the do-gooder mandarins of the Health and Safety department and dismissed the issue with a quiet 'feck 'em'.

Small jack pike fed voraciously throughout the morning, spiralling up through the dirty water and attacking our rattlers and minnows just below the surface. We all caught and were grateful for the smallest of fish after three days on land. Teddy, at Ricky's request, had changed the spark plugs on his outboard to facilitate a slower trolling speed, in the hope that a big old trout might bite. It didn't happen and so the morning passed as it had on Monday, with Teddy's accounts of scandal and intrigue.

We were told legends of the hill-dwellers, folk tales of the ancients and more contemporary stories about those we had drunk with all week in the Whiskey Still. No one, from old Leinster kings to the village policeman, escaped Teddy's good-natured gossip. They were all bastards or thieves, he told us, and deserved their slagging. When he ran out of Irishmen to curse, he started on us. We laughed and fished and ignored the worsening rain, and it was mid-morning before we noticed that the lough was developing an ominous chop. I was holding on to my rod so as not to miss any subtle trout bites, and as lunch approached I noticed that my knuckles were white from the cold. Teddy noticed, too, and for Anna's benefit muttered, 'he's a keen fisherman, that boy'. It was not a compliment but a warning, though neither of us realised until much, much later.

By midday we had worked the northern bays and crossed to the southern shoreline near Ryan's Point. Teddy steered the boat to a wooded island and tied up, and four wet and luckless trout hunters gathered for lunch beneath a canopy of oak and beech. The food was soaked through, but Ricky and I had brought our Kelly Kettles with us. These primitive boiling engines could produce four pints of frothing water in only minutes using a handful of twigs or a sheet of newspaper, and even our boatman was impressed. He was also quick to inform us of their Irish heritage. 'They were invented by the ghillies on Lough Conn a hundred years ago,' we were told, 'and they're not called Kelly fekkin' kettles. Those there are County Mayo volcanoes.'

Ricky and I had heard numerous stories about our kettles over the years, but whether they were first boiled by fishermen, railway navvies or farmers, every account located their origins to Ireland's west coast. It felt good to fire them up and pop their corks in the land of their birth, and the coffee we drank was exquisite. Our body temperatures rose and, though this did much to revive our spirits for the final afternoon, there was an air of disquiet among us – time was short, the trout invisible and the lough itself in malevolent mood. In the next twenty-four hours there would be a long drive across Ireland and another ferry trip to endure.

Anna tidied the camp and stamped out the fire. We checked our lines, changed our lures and my cousin injected his insulin in readiness for a difficult final afternoon. The wind and rain had both worsened and we knew that the weather would force us back to Dromineer before long.

The light had also dropped and I was concerned for Ricky; it was all too easy to forget that my fishing partner was a blind man on a foreign lough without a life jacket, and that I had promised his wife and son I would take care of him. It was during our shore lunch that I began to recognise the toll this ferox hunt was taking on my cousin, though he brushed aside all comment; it would be years before either of us would do much about it.

Ricky's diabetes had long been problematic; his years as a ghillie and long periods working on the oil rigs at Nigg had been tough on his kidneys, and the teenager who had led my brother and I from river to loch and back again was now a prematurely old man. Before Teddy pushed us back out on to the water, I thought briefly about Fran and Michael who were waiting in Alness for Ricky to return and hoped he would have a good story to share with them.

Teddy steered us to new waters in the next three hours. The increasing chop made the open lough perilous and some semblance of calm could be found between the islands on the southern bank. We weaved slowly between them, casting our lighter lures over the shallower areas and trolling them when there was sufficient depth. The pike were as active as they had been in the morning and we were soon among small jacks. Later, we left the islands and began to work the open waters on the way back to Dromineer. The pike disappeared and a south-westerly that had found greater strength with every passing hour caught us broadside. All our boat-man's skills were needed to keep us on a straight course, as water began to roll over the clinker's bow and accumulate at our feet. A whispered debate began among the three of us about whether Teddy should make for shore, but all of us were reluctant to offend our sage. He was a skilled captain, the best on Derg, and there was always the possibility that our fears were exaggerated.

While Ricky and Anna and I exchanged glances, something happened which surprised us all. My Lane Minnow was intercepted once more, but differently. There was no familiar quarter-circling of the rod, as there had been with every pike; no relentless unmissable resistance, just a pluck, a shake, a third brief enquiry and then silence. I struck, but the unseen cause had vanished as quickly as it had arrived. We discussed it excitedly. Weed perhaps? A bigger pike? No, said Teddy, that had been a trout, and perhaps a big one. We would never know the truth of it, but our ghillie was unequivocal and closed the matter with some fine west coast logic: 'No trout would take a lure until the mayflies were up. Never. But they're contrary feckers, and if one lost his head and did, that's just how he'd take it.'

We fished on and the weather deteriorated. Water continued to breach the bow and thoughts of missed trout were replaced by a palpable concern for safety. Teddy made the decision for us, as a captain should, and declared the day's fishing to be over. Rods were disassembled, lures put away and the boat pointed towards Dromineer for the last time. Fifteen minutes later we arrived at the quay and could reflect upon our missed chance from the safety of dry land.

Frank was there, smoking a cigarette in the last light, as our boat drifted in. We passed him our rods and bags and stepped ashore, and stood blowing warm air through our fingers as he told us the news of the day. While we had been out on the lough, politicians from both sides of the Irish Sea, and from seemingly irreconcilable sides of a sectarian divide, had put their names to a Good Friday Agreement. If the day's fishing had been unremarkable, it mattered not. The country had taken a significant step towards peace that day and we felt fortunate just to be on Irish waters and among its people – the trout could wait for another time.

Frank was delighted, Teddy too, but our suggestion of a pint in celebration was not well received. With the solemnity of a cardinal, the landlord declared that this was Good Friday, and that meant one thing above all others: his pub was closed, all pubs were closed, and Ireland was dry.

Our boatman was thirsty and took up the cause. He protested, charmed, called for a recount and demanded dispensation from the Vatican, but Frank was unimpressed and walked away. 'There are other pubs,' Teddy declared, and marched up the slipway towards the town. We followed him.

There were indeed other pubs and other landlords, and Teddy seemed to know them all, but wherever we went our money was refused and his papist credentials questioned. Nobody in Dromineer would serve us. Within an hour we knew we were unwelcome in

Portroe, Ballyhogan and Puckane. Finally, Anna's car took us to Nenagh and there we found a small hotel with its bar lights glowing. It was open for food and would serve us a drink if we sat down to eat. This, Teddy assured us, was entirely within the spirit of Good Friday. Refusal was tantamount to heresy and, moreover, a challenge to Anglo-Irish relations. We opened our wallets and sat down for one final evening with the wise old man of Derg.

The barman took our drinks order and informed us that all meals were fixed at a set price of 20 punts. We agreed without knowing if we had enough money left and rummaged for the last of our change while the black stuff was poured. By the time it arrived, our pockets were empty and 80 punts lay on the table in a desperate pile of crumpled notes and small coins. The barman scooped it all into his apron without counting and turned to leave. We called him back and asked for a menu.

'Jesus, lads, I'm sorry, did you not know today is Good Friday?' he replied. 'We'll not be cooking tonight.'

The three of us left Dromineer at dawn the next day and within hours were boarding the ferry for the mainland. Ireland had surrendered none of its fabled monsters and the weather had kept us from its waters for all but two days. We were penniless and hungry. Ricky was especially drained by the experience and would need a period of quiet recovery before he could cast again.

New plans were discussed on the ferry crossing. I would return to the Highlands in the summer and we would fish Shin, Veyatie and Kildermorie. Anna suggested she might join us but I tried to discourage her; there would be no Gaelic charm, no nights among the black stuff, no waterside cottages or slate mines in Scotland. The fishing would be relentless, the environment hostile and the days long. I suggested we return to Ireland the following spring and hunt the giants of the Galway loughs. There were hotels for us to stay in and ghillies we could hire. We could explore castles and eat in white stone pubs and do the things that young couples do. But Anna was headstrong and wanted to see the Highlands and so our crew increased by one.

10

THE BIG FELLOW

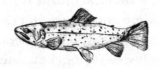

On a Saturday in the last week of May, Anna and I drove to Scotland. Ricky had recovered from Ireland and Teddy and our nights in the Whiskey Still, and had arranged boats on Veyatie and Kildermorie. Anna had heard so much about Loch Shin and was keen to fish there too, but above all was looking forward to showing the boys how it should be done. Neither of us doubted that she would.

The ten-hour journey passed quickly with Anna for company, but as we drove north there were moments of silence and I thought about the year that had passed since the capture of our first ferox trout. Roo was gone for reasons I could well understand, Martin for reasons unknown and more than one credit card company was keen to know my whereabouts. My brother had moved halfway across the world, and I was approaching my thirties with little to show for it in any conventional sense. A rational man might have questioned it all, but I did not. None of it felt important – Ricky and I were closer than ever, I had a new girlfriend and there were giant trout waiting to be caught. If problems in Wiltshire became insurmountable, I would hide in the mountains until they no longer mattered.

Gordy would not be joining us for the week. He had found some work as a rat-catcher and his free time was promised to a new girl who, Fran delighted in telling us, was a tattoo artist with elaborately decorated skin and pierced nipples. Such exotic ladies were rarer in the Highlands than ferox trout and I silently approved his new priorities. He could always return to us when the ink ran dry.

We arrived late on Saturday and knew that Shin was forbidden to us the following day, but Ricky had made arrangements with the keeper on Loch Veyatie. For the price of a bottle of malt whisky and a bag of sweets for his bairns, centuries of puritan tradition could be overruled, and we would have the loch to ourselves on Sunday. In reality, this meant we had the keys to the gate at the top of the path into the loch and a second key to unlock the padlocked boat. After that we were on our own, with no legitimacy in the eyes of the bailiffs or higher authorities. Wrathful vengeance was a distinct possibility; Veyatie was, after all, the loch that bestowed its greatest prizes on men of the cloth. But, all other waters were closed and there was little else to do, and so we decided to risk damnation.

The loch was even more beautiful than I remembered. It was still late spring on the west coast and heather was just appearing on the slopes of Suilven and Cul Mor. There was no rain this time, no strong Atlantic winds to scupper us, and it seemed that our heresy was being politely ignored. Neither God nor the bailiffs questioned our presence and we enjoyed calm water all day. Good fortune was with us and we all caught trout on deep-diving yellow plugs, though the biggest one weighed only 2lb. As it lay in the landing net, the fish regurgitated its breakfast – a 4-inch charr – and any doubts about the predatory credentials of Veyatie trout were forgotten. The monsters lurking beneath the Black Falls failed to materialise, but we had seen enough to know that we should return, albeit on a day when our presence might be blessed.

As we drove back over the mountains to Alness in darkness, Ricky suggested that we increase the size of the lures we were using in an effort to raise the larger fish. Anna proposed that we start wearing dog collars instead. We were buoyant and optimistic and thought we had got away with it.

Vengeance in the Highlands may come late, but it doesn't pull its punches. The following two days were wet and squally with winds of over 20mph. We tried to get afloat on Shin, but could only troll the waters near the angling club for short periods before the clinker started to fill up or our boat was pushed to shore. Further out, the waves were white-capped and over 3ft high, and the far shoreline was obscured by sheet rain and mist. The romance of Ireland and nights in Frank's bar seemed very distant and when I managed to drop the winding button of my new wristwatch overboard, the girl who had bought it for me seemed a little distant, too. Of course, we caught nothing.

On our fourth morning Ricky received a call from Ian, one of the keepers on the Novar Estate. Kildermorie was suffering the same high winds and they would not allow us to use their boat until it had subsided. Shin would be just as tempestuous and there seemed little point in driving north into Sutherland until the gales had passed. Fran pointed out that Ricky would benefit from a day of good food, regular insulin and dry land, and so we decamped to Inverness.

I wanted to show Anna the town where I was born. It seemed like the sort of meaningful, poignant thing that proper boyfriends did, though in truth I was as much a stranger there as she was. We looked at the spot where the old Raigmore Maternity Ward had been, where boredom had driven my mother to smoking as she waited for her twins to arrive, but the buildings had changed in thirty years and there was little to see. I hadn't imagined there would be a plaque or statue, but I had expected to feel a connection of sorts. Nothing about it resonated; there was no sense of familiarity or belonging, and I realised that Scotland for me was about summer holidays and Alness and Ricky's half of the family, and that my birth in its northernmost city was not part of its magic. The flat riverside landscape and urban sprawl seemed at odds with the Scotland I was trying to reclaim, and so we gave up trying to find meaning where there was none and accepted Ricky's offer to take us to the finest fishing tackle shop in the Highlands.

Graham's of Castle Street occupied a three-storey Victorian terrace in the old city centre. When we entered it smelt of mucilin, varnish and waxed cotton, as proper tackle shops should. There were vintage rods and reels on display – including a right-handed Hardy Altex which was sadly not for sale – and trays of hand-tied salmon flies on the wooden counter. Yellowing photographs of customers with fish of all sizes were stuck to the walls, and among the racks of carbon weapons were some fine examples of bamboo. There were concessions to modernity – echo sounders and electronic bite alarms for the pike fishermen – but in all other respects it reminded me of the shops I had frequented in England in the 1970s, before the invasion of camouflaged bivouacs and chemical baits. I loved the place immediately. We bought some lures and, in an act of unjustified optimism, a new set of scales, and lingered until Anna became restless.

Before leaving Inverness, Ricky insisted that we also visit Leakey's, a second-hand bookshop in a renovated church. It was reputed to be the largest of its kind in Scotland, though its owner had rightly prioritised ambience over gigantism and it felt as intimate as a private library. If the tackle shop had offered comfort on a fishless day, Leakey's offered a timely reminder of the history and landscape in which we had immersed ourselves. One corner was given over to antiquated maps of the Highlands, but everywhere else it seemed that piles of books were holding the building itself together. Most were old, and alongside classics were volumes by Scottish naturalists, poets and countrymen. It was quite wonderful. There was an alcove dedicated to angling books and we raided it with reckless disregard for our overdrafts. There was also a café at the top of a spiral staircase and we raided that as well.

Our day of rest grew darker and colder and so we drove north, stopping in Dingwall for cigarettes on the road back to Alness. As Anna and I stood puffing in the High Street, Ricky remembered an antique shop that we might enjoy and led us to it. Like the

Ludgershall shop that I passed every day, this place was a dimly lit cave of eccentricity. There were farming tools, piles of crockery, portraits of long-gone lairds and ladies, and countless items of fishy interest. On the second floor I found an umbrella stand full of rods, including a Walker Mk IV Avon and two Scotties salmon spinning rods. If Anna hadn't been standing next to me I would have taken them all.

On the ground floor was a cabinet of old reels: Hardy Perfects, Allcocks Starbacks, Bakelite centrepins and rusted fixed spools. Each was priced sensibly and I knew that if the same items had been in Simon's shop we would have sold them for double. As I examined them, Anna explored the books. More classics were found, including a first edition of Dick Walker's opus, *Stillwater Angling*. Inside, the first owner had written a shopping list: 'size 4 model perfects, 12lb Platil, Arlesey bombs, loaf of bread' – all essential items for a fifties carp man. I wondered how the book had ended up in Dingwall and whether its first owner had walked away from the carp pools of southern England on his own Scottish odyssey.

The shopkeeper was a garrulous sort and an angler to boot; we talked of charr and of the giant trout that ate them until it was time for him to close up. It was only when we were about to leave that he appeared to remember something. 'Did you not see the big fellow upstairs?' he asked. Puzzled, we said we had not and so he led us to the second floor. There, behind the rods and hidden by a bookcase, was a stuffed fish. Old age and mould had taken their toll, but the huge frame of a 15lb ferox trout was unmistakable. The creature was mounted on a wooden board and there was no inscription, but the owner knew a little of its history: 'It's nearly 100 years old, and I got it from one of the hotels when it got too tatty to be on show. I can't be certain, but I believe it came from Kildermorie.' We drove home in darkness, more optimistic than ever.

Later that evening, Ricky took a call from Ian the Keeper. Another big fellow upstairs had forgiven us and the winds on the hills of the Novar Estate had weakened. The waters on Kildermorie had calmed and the boat was ours if we wanted it. In the morning we would return to a loch I hadn't seen in eighteen years.

11

KILDERMORIE

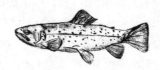

Loch Kildermorie, like so many of its kind, is found at the end of a long un-made road which sees traffic only from estate workers and fishermen, and precious few of them. The road into Kildermorie snakes up the mountains of Easter Ross, leaving behind the coastal flatness of Alness, before entering the heavily forested lands of the Novar Estate. The water itself is ancient and the landscape older still.

The loch is the smaller of two that feed the rivers of this part of Cromarty, but this smallness is relative; Kildermorie, like its sister Loch Glass, is deep, dark and huge. Both are part of a topography whose story began 3 billion years ago. To stand on the shores of this glacial wilderness, surrounded by heather-clad mountains and rocks and forest, is to experience the geological essence of the Scottish Highlands. And yet few would know that every molecule of it is on a northward journey which began at the other end of the world.

The land that became Scotland was once part of a forgotten continent called Laurentia, deep in the southern Atlantic. It rode the tectonic plates for millions of years as the earth formed and shifted, enduring every extreme of climate and circumstance and eventually breaking up to contribute to the land masses we know as Greenland and North America. Before the later ice ages, Scotland was at different times a desert and a tropical swamp, a lifeless volcanic hell and an ocean floor. Its present stark beauty has been hard-won.

Beneath it all lies the bedrock and this also has a story to tell. Scotland's foundations consist broadly of five distinct types, but in ferox country there are two: the Lewisian gneisses of the north-west, on which the Torrodonian sandstone of Veyatie sits; and to the east a larger expanse known to geologists as the Moine Supergroup. This billion-year-old formation of deposited sands and muds from an ancient ocean sits beneath much of the Highlands. Above, the scouring and compressing of the ice ages built the landscape we know now – the mountains and the lochs, the valleys and peaks, the cool deep water – and thus a world in which giant trout could thrive.

Kildermorie, like Glass and Shin, runs north-west to south-east, and its cold waters flow into the Alness River. The loch is both deep and wide, but feels intimate; the mountains that encircle it slope steeply, particularly on the northern shore, and the heavy forestry of the estate adds to a sense of claustrophobia and darkness. The lodge is found by its north-westerly tip at Abhainn na Glasa, but elsewhere there is little sign of human life. A wind farm overlooks the southern shore, but in all other respects Kildermorie remains an untouched wilderness; just another loch in a timeless landscape whose story has been unfolding for a billion years, and whose conclusion is too far away to comprehend.

Man's role in this tale has been minimal and brief. Until the second millennium, the hills and lochs were all but ignored, the trout neglected, and few souls would have ventured into the highlands of Easter Ross. The lands of Novar would have offered sanctuary only to those whose circumstances had taken them outside the simple, ordered life of the villages – criminals and wayward husbands, papists and revolutionaries. The remoter Highlands were a land for the damned and the banished.

It took a remarkable individual to embrace the landscape of Kildermorie, but in the 1760s such a man arrived. Hector Munro was a celebrated army major, winning honours in India and leading the fight against Jacobite rebels closer to home. Whilst abroad his two sons were killed, one by a tiger, the other by a shark, and in the 1760s he returned to Scotland with the less hapless members of his family. Munro became MP for the Burgh of Inverness and inheritor of the lands between Loch Glass and Alness. There, he oversaw the construction of Novar House and conscripted local men to flatten the unruly land around it. With the family seat completed, Munro turned his attentions to the mountains and waters that came with his title, and oversaw the creation of an estate that survives to this day. However, the old major didn't forget his time in the subcontinent and, in a nod to his Indian endeavours, ordered the building of the Fyrish Monument overlooking Alness in 1782. The chain of stone arches erected at the summit could be seen from every house in Alness, every farm and settlement along the Cromarty coast, and mirrored styles Munro had seen in the subcontinent. The project provided much-needed work for local villagers and secured his immortality in that wild corner of Scotland. And yet, even the efforts of one such as Hector Munro could not bring order to the hills above Novar House; Kildermorie remained a place where the laws of nature outweighed those of man.

When Anna's car descended the final yards to the bay where our boat was moored, the water appeared before us and we both gasped. I had, of course, been here many years ago but we were on the opposite shore from the one on which Ricky and I had once strung up our rods with bubble floats and worms. It took a moment to recalibrate my memories and then it was unmistakably the loch where my cousin had taught me to fish. The peak of Meall Mor rose above the far bank, tufts of heather claimed patches of earth among the grey rock of the slopes, and beneath it all lay Kildermorie – still, dimpled with rising trout, clear in its margins and impossibly deep where the valley plunged to its prehistoric origins. Throughout the years I had spent in England –

the years in which Ricky had grown up and become a father and been saved by a surgeon's knife – it was here where I had always pictured him, threading worms on lines and repelling the midgies with camp fires and Embassy No 5s. Anna declared it gorgeous and suggested we get the boat fixed up for some fishing. Ricky and I were less hurried and inhaled the landscape with slow, deep breaths. This place was the bedrock of our past, too.

By mid-morning we were fishing. The mooring was at the loch's end where still water turned to river and so we trolled north-west and back again, exploring the margins and zig-zagging across to the far bank when the mood took. Ricky used the small yellow plug that had proven so effective on Veyatie, while Anna and I experimented with lures that promised to emulate the colours and movements of the small trout and charr. We fished until dusk, stopping only once for food and insulin. For the first hour Ricky and I introduced Anna to Kildermorie's most obvious landmarks: the curious circle of stones at the river's source, the bay where we had fished as boys and the charred stumps where the boathouse had once stood. Later, we prospected the water below the lodge, which had been tantalisingly out of reach all those summers ago.

Ricky was always a garrulous skipper, but on our first day on Kildermorie he had more to say than usual. My cousin had worked the upper beats of the Averon in his youth, guiding visiting salmon fishers from one beat to another, and a morning at the river's source was enough to stir his memories. We laughed all afternoon at stories of American tourists with creels full of dollars, plum-voiced Englishmen who barely knew which end of the rod to hold and who believed that salmon could be conjured up by wearing their old school tie, and at Ricky's run-ins with poachers, most of whom were his childhood friends. Later, as the sun dipped and the temperature fell, Ricky's reminiscing turned to wistfulness, and he talked about family and the grandfather I had never known.

Andrew 'Baldy' Fraser, my mother's father, died of bowel cancer five years before my brother and I were born and his life had long been a mystery to me. He was rarely mentioned at home and the two grandparents who survived long enough to know Chris and I were more than enough to be getting on with. It was only when I returned to Scotland and to Ricky that I began to ask questions and on that calm Kildermorie evening Ricky began to answer them.

Andrew Fraser earned his nickname as a young boy, when his mother sent him down Alness high street for a haircut. He and a pal spent the money on sweets and performed the scalping themselves, to the anger of my great-grandmother Johanna and the amusement of everyone else. The name stuck and he was Baldy for the rest of his days. He was a rogue, a scamp and a charmer with a drink in him – and those too smart to fall for his chat were entertained by his musical prowess with the mouth organ and penny whistle. Baldy also played the biggest drum of them all in the local distillery bands, the one with the loudest boom and leopard-skin accessories, and this was typical of him. The people of Alness always knew when Baldy was around. In 1940 he dutifully marched out of Alness with his mates in the Seaforth Highlanders to take on Hitler, but was captured at St Valery and spent five years as a prisoner of war in an Eastern European Stalag. Later, Ricky would show me the two surviving photographs of Baldy from those years. In both he is grinning widely and clutching his penny whistle, but few who knew him doubted that the Nazis stole his finest years.

Within a year of his return, my mother Valerie was born. By then, Baldy was an older and more embittered man; his war had been easier than it might have been, but it had done him little good all the same.

He was, to use the polite euphemism of the day, a ladies' man, but he was also a grafter. Baldy Fraser worked the bars in Alness, served as nightwatchman at local distilleries and was the village chimney sweep. It was astonishing that he found time for carousing, but he did.

I was delighted to learn from Ricky that my grandfather was among the gangs that had built the hydroelectric dam on Shin in the 1950s and it was this revelation that drew me closer to him.

The concrete edifice at Shin had provided the backdrop to our ferox hunt, but I hadn't known that my grandfather's hands had once toiled there in the unforgiving Highland climate.

I knew my mother's family a little better by the end of the day. My grandmother Christina, Baldy's wife, had been an old lady when we had holidayed with her as children. I remembered only her white hair and bronchial laugh, her frequent offerings of jam-filled floury baps, which she called 'pieces', and the love she had for my father and for Chris and I. The more I learnt of Baldy, the better I understood her bent-backed, long-suffering gait and her devotion to the non-carousing man who whisked her daughter away. I wondered briefly whether I, as a hopeless boyfriend with a fondness for malt and tobacco, had inherited some of the old man's questionable ways. If Anna asked herself the same question, she was kind enough not to say.

Ricky steered the outboard towards the mouth of the loch as the last of the light went, cutting the engine as we drifted silently over the shallows towards the mooring. The water beneath us was black. Rods and bags were packed away and finally the fish we had caught were celebrated. We had landed a few that day, and though none deserved immortality in Kildermorie Lodge, they were big enough for us.

We drove down into Alness in darkness and spent the final hours of the day raising toasts to Kildermorie and to family, to Hector and his luckless sons, to the dam-builders and the foresters and to anyone else who'd left their mark on that timeless landscape. And on that evening we knew that we were a tiny part of it, too. Just molecules drifting aimlessly on the bedrock, perhaps, but part of it all the same.

12

THE TYROS

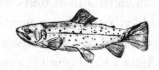

Ricky, the Alness boys and I knew we were part of a very small group of anglers with an interest in catching ferox and we rather liked it that way. We never saw anybody else trolling for them on Shin or Kildermorie or Veyatie – not one – and when we mentioned them in tackle shops or to other anglers, responses could vary from antipathy to disbelief.

'Big lake troot? Cannibals? Are ye' sure your no' thinking of pike?'

'Fer … wha'? No, none o' them here, only brownies.'

'Thieving ugly bastards, m' pal told me he saw one eat three ducklings.'

That sort of thing. Occasionally, we met other anglers who had tried for them, or knew someone who had, or who had heard about crazy scientists further south who caught them with sonar equipment and scuba gear and, quite possibly, lasers; but it did seem that ferox fishing in the remoter north was an all but forgotten sport.

We weren't alone, but our nearest comrades-in-rods were the Ferox 85 group, who fished on Awe, Quoich and Rannoch. We had heard that there was a small community of ferox enthusiasts on these waters and that they could be counted in dozens, not hundreds. I could have met more anglers in a single day at a popular carp lake.

But it wasn't always so. The sporting literature of the Highlands suggested that ferox fishing had its own golden age and that we had missed it by fifty years. It began in the earliest days of the railways, when the Far North Line opened up Perthshire and beyond, and ended when men marched away to the Second World War and big trout didn't seem to matter anymore. By then, the writers of the age had declared the lochs over-fished and the ferox in decline, and the Führer was judged a more worthy adversary.

Half a century would pass before ferox were rediscovered by anglers in their numbers and, when they were, the writings of the old masters were unearthed. The fish's habits were as mercurial as ever and so the methods employed borrowed much from men like Charles St John, P.D. Malloch and the incomparable John Colquhoun. We knew that the Pitlochry men had read them and Ricky and I turned to them too, though their books were almost as hard to find as the fish themselves.

W.G.C. St John wrote of ferox in *Wild Sports of the Highlands* (1888) and gave a detailed account of trolling on Loch Awe. His account confirmed how little had changed:

The only way to kill a larger trout is by trolling. In Loch Awe and several other lochs I have seen this kind of fishing succeed well. If the sportsman is skilful, he is sure of taking finer trout in this way than he would ever do when fly fishing. In trolling there are two or three rules which should be carefully observed:-

Choose the roughest wind that your boat can live in; fish with a good-sized bait, not much less than a herring, and do not commence your trolling till after two-o-clock in the afternoon, by which time the large fish seem to have digested their last night's supper and to be again on the move. You may pass over the heads of hundreds of large trout when they are lying at rest and not hungry, and you will not catch one; but as soon as they begin to feed, a fish, though he may have half a dozen small trout in his stomach, will still run at your bait. The weight of the sinkers on your line and the depth at which you fish must of course depend on the depth of the water in the loch. A patient fisherman should find out how deep every reach and bay is before he begins to troll. The labour of a day spent in taking soundings is well repaid. The strength and activity of the large loch trout is immense, and he will run out your whole reel-line if allowed to do so. Sometimes he will go down perpendicularly to the bottom, where he remains sulky or attempts to rub off the hooks: get him out of this situation and away he goes, almost towing your boat after him. This is the time for your boatman to make play to keep up with the fish and save your line, for a salmo ferox is no ignoble foe to contend with when you have him at the end of a common fishing line: he appears to have the strength of a whale as he rushes away.

John Colquhoun was born in Edinburgh in March 1805. His father was Sir James Colquhoun of Luss, chief of the Clan Colquhoun, and his mother was an equally formidable character, highly regarded in religious circles and held great sway over the family. John Colquhoun was educated by private tutors and spent much of his childhood on the banks of Loch Lomond. According to his eldest daughter, the young Colquhoun and his brothers were encouraged to pursue their interest in the natural world; non-poisonous snakes were sent as gifts from family friends in England, while the boys' schoolrooms were embellished with stuffed reptiles and birds. It was small wonder that Colquhoun would grow up a prodigious hunter, naturalist and angler.

His thoughts on all things wild and Scottish – from deer-driving in Mull to the feral cats of Ben Cruachan – were recorded in *The Moor and the Loch*, which was published by Blackwood and Sons in several editions between the 1830s and 1885. In it, Colquhoun

wrote at length about the sport which, it could be said, he popu-
larised: loch fishing for *salmo ferox*.

Greer mentioned him frequently and so Ricky and I were
keen to obtain a copy of his opus. When we did we were not
disappointed. Ours was a seventh edition and was inscribed by
a previous owner: *J. W. Fogg Elliot, Durham 1893*. The frontispiece
recorded a price of 5 shillings, but we were obliged to pay rather
more.

The book included a photograph of the author, glued into an
early page, and so we at last knew what a ferox tyro looked like.
Colquhoun was slight, suited in tweed with a cravat and trilby;
he had curly white hair and the kind of elaborate moustache that
just isn't seen anymore. His chest was puffed out with a degree of
arrogance, but when we had finished reading his chapters on ferox
fishing we knew he had every right to display a little pride. We
read his words repeatedly, and his wisdom became our own:

> Trolling for giant trout is the very acme of rod-fishing. It is gen-
> erally thought that the whole of this exciting sport consists in
> fixing good baits upon the trolling-rod, letting out a sufficiency
> of line, and mainly relying upon the boatman's skill to point out
> the best fishing ground. Although trolling after this fashion may
> occasionally be successful, yet the reverse is far oftener experi-
> enced, when all the blame is sure to be laid on the weather, as
> the best ground has been searched and the baits were excellent.
> Few gentlemen are aware how easily this best ground may be
> changed to a good distance on either side, by a bright sun, a
> breeze of wind, or a rise of the loch after rain. This is invariably
> the case where the shores are level, and the depth consequently
> gradual. Should the sky be dark and the loch discoloured, or, on
> the contrary, small and clear with a cloudless sky, a difference in
> the size and colour of the bait, and rapidity in spinning it, may
> bring home an empty boat or reward us with a couple of trout
> that will give the boatman as much trouble to carry as two buck-
> ets of water.

There are three kinds of trout that peculiarly belong to this description of fishing. And, first, the great salmo ferox, from its size, strength and cunning deserves the highest place ... [In] trolling for any of these fish, especially for the salmo ferox, great attention should be paid to the tackle, not only that it is all of the very best quality, but that it is dressed in the manner that is least apt to miss the trout. Of course the angler must not expect many runs in a day, which makes it particularly vexatious when the fish that do dash at the bait escape the hooks. Of course, when trolling for the feroxes, all the hooks must be very large.

When fairly afloat, beware of trusting too implicitly to your boatman, even should you be totally unacquainted with the loch. It commonly happens, unless he is a good practical fisher, that he will take you over the same ground under all circumstances, and should no fish run, lay the blame on something unpropitious in the day, which it may require some ingenuity on his part to discover, and some credulity on yours to believe. Your best plan with such a guide is to make him be most particular about the surest resorts of the large fish; and should you be unsuccessful the first time of going over them, try again a little nearer the shore, if there is much wind; or, if it be calm, a little further out, especially when the loch is small. Towards dusk you may generally keep nearer the shore, also when the loch has risen or is discoloured from rain. You must not then sink the baits so deep, but raise them by taking off some of the sinking lead – not by winding up a part of the line, as the shallower you troll the more need of a long line.

The best time of year for the salmo ferox is the end of April, May, and the beginning of June. They are very dormant all July and August, particularly if the weather be hot. Although much more shy than in spring, they sometimes take pretty fair in September.

Never find fault with the boatman, when the hooks stick fast, for taking you in to too shallow water. If they do, they will be most likely to prevent this annoyance, by keeping too deep for any fish to see your bait. Most guides are too apt, at any rate, to err this way, to save themselves trouble, as they dread a fast even more than the angler. The truth is, when trolling for salmo ferox, the baits should be hung only a few yards from the bottom. Be assured that the largest fish are generally taken by trolling close to the bottom, as they are lazy.

Colquhoun listed several impressive catches to his rods: nine fish to 10lb in a week on Loch Awe, two 12lb fish from Awe on one autumn day, nine fish to 14lb in a week from Loch Layghal in Sutherland and a 17lb monster to a fly from the head of the River Awe. We envied him the time he had to pursue them – Colquhoun enjoyed the leisurely pace of the moneyed classes and could indulge his love of the sport with little fear of bankruptcy or divorce – but we also knew that he went afloat without echo sounders, waterproof neoprene or life jackets. He had no car to take him to the edge of the loch, no outboard motor to rush him to the best water. His catches would have been noteworthy in any era, but in the middle years of Victoria's reign, they were astonishing.

In the year that Baldy Fraser marched out of Alness and into the hands of the Nazis, a small Edinburgh company published the first book to consider ferox trout and their prey in scientific terms. I was told about it by the same Welsh bookseller who had sold me Greer's and Colquhoun's works, and he was even able to supply me with a copy. The bookseller was canny and knew that my interest in ferox was spiralling beyond reason and I was sure this was reflected in the book's high price. It didn't stop me from buying it.

The author was R.P. Hardie, and his *Ferox and Charr in the Lochs of Scotland – an Inquiry* listed geological and scientific data for almost every water known to hold either or both species. Hardie's book was intended as the first of two, but the second was never completed and so his research omitted the far north; nonetheless, it added considerably to our growing list of ferox lochs.

Hardie used the same texts that Ricky and I had tracked down – Stoddart, Colquhoun and Houghton – but he also used the *Bathymetrical Survey of the Freshwater Lochs of Scotland* (1910) and other geological sources. He divided his coverage into ten regions, from southern Scotland to Ewe and Gairloch, and listed over 250 lochs. Many of these seemed to contain only charr and the smaller trouts, but at least half of those listed were said to have ferox populations to a greater or lesser degree. For Ricky and me, it was mesmerising stuff, but details on the lochs we had already fished were scant.

Of Kildermorie, Hardie had the following to say:

Loch Morie is 2½ miles in length, and 622 feet above the sea. The greatest depth is 270 feet, and the mean depth is 125 feet, which is about 46.3 per cent of the former. The slope of the bottom is in some places very steep – for instance, off the southern shore, where a sounding of 75 feet was taken about 60 feet from the shore, and one of 124 feet about 120 feet from the shore, showing a gradient exceeding 1 in 1. There are ordinary trout and ferox in the loch, and there are (or were) many charr, but no salmon.

On Shin, he was barely more effusive:

The scenery of Loch Shin is rather tame, but the view looking up the loch to Ben More Assynt is very fine. The length of the loch measured along its centre is about 17¼ miles. The floor of the loch is very irregular, and the figures given by the Bathymetrical Survey show that it is comparatively shallow, 58 per cent of the lake floor being covered by less than 50 feet of water, and 85 per cent by less than 100 feet of water, while the area deeper than 150 feet of water is extremely small. The greatest depth is 162 feet, and the mean depth 51 feet. Loch Shin is a very good ferox loch, and the ordinary trout are of rather fine quality, averaging nearly ½lb. The loch contains some charr.

Hardie's research was conducted before the building of Loch Shin's hydroelectric dam, which added almost 2 miles to its length and much to its depth, so we accepted that some of his information would be incorrect. I hadn't bought the book for its scientific accuracy anyway; I had bought it because the bookseller had been smart enough to wave it under my nose.

Ferox and Charr in the Lochs of Scotland offered nothing new in terms of fishing methods, but the accounts of old monsters proved inspirational and so it did not matter. Hardie recorded that in 1800 Baron Norton caught a 30-pounder from Loch Rannoch, and that a Major Cheape took a 21-pounder from the same water later in the century. Loch Leven was said to have given up trout in excess of 18lb and Quoich one of 26lb. Loch Ness was said to have produced at least one ferox of similar size.

Every one of these historic fish exceeded the official British Record (rod-caught) Fish Committee's brown trout record, but in every instance the monsters had been caught in the distant past. The captures could not be verified retrospectively and had been discarded long ago by the list-makers. Ricky and I were less cynical; the Victorians were perfectly capable of weighing fish and there was no reason to doubt them. Hardie's book did much to confirm our view that the golden age of ferox trout had passed us by.

That didn't matter either. Mr Hardie had omitted Veyatie and the other lochs of remoter Sutherland and knew nothing of their secrets. He had been peering into the depths with the clinical view of a scientist. We, on the other hand, were simple anglers and the size of fish we hoped for was limited only by our imaginations. Hardie's book told us all that we needed to know; the ferox were out there and could be found in many more lochs than we had first supposed. The majority of these places were no longer fished for their ferox, if indeed they ever were, and they all had the depth and shoals of prey fish required to grow a monster. We didn't need bathymetrical surveys to tell us that there was magic below the surface. All we had to do was go fishing.

One of the last great ferox tyros was R. Macdonald Robertson. Like the others, he was a salmon and trout man, a fly fisherman who was willing to abandon tradition when the chance of a monster arose. His greatest story appeared in *In Scotland with a Fishing Rod* (1935), and was called 'Tussle with a Salmo Ferox':

We were sitting lazily chatting and striving to combat the delightful lassitude induced by hard exercise on a stormy loch, followed by the luxury of a change to the skin, a hearty dinner and a crackling log fire. It was mid-September, and the equinoctial gales appeared to have set in permanently, accompanied by lashing rain, which was causing the loch to rise rapidly. To us was announced Nichol Macintyre, our boatman, who for more than forty years had materially assisted in thinning the piscine inhabitants of Loch Awe, and who could never be induced to lay down oars until all hope of 'adding a fin to the gentleman's creel' had vanished. We were in the dining room of the Auchnacarron Lodge, on the north shore of Loch Awe, when Macintyre entered. He suggested that we should next day try the river; we must start about eight o' clock, as we had seven miles to pull, and, if the gale held from the west, it would take all we knew to pull the three miles to the Pass.

Next morning I was awoken by a shower of gravel. Tumbling in to my clothes, I hurried downstairs, and put up a substantial lunch, while breakfast was being prepared. By eight o' clock we were ready to start.

Wet work it was getting an offing, but when once clear of the shore, we had the wind dead aft and a clear run of four miles before us. I sent Nichol forward to trim the boat, and then, with the sheet in one hand, and an extemporized tiller in the other, our little craft, with the aid of a tiny lugsail, performed the run in half an hour. Having reached the entrance to the Pass of Brander, we crept up the weather shore with a minnow on my salmon rod and an ordinary trout cast and flies on my trouting rod. On reaching the last sheltered point I took in my minnow, but allowed the flies to remain out with a very short line. We then settled down to a hard pull.

When we had gone about another mile and had reached the part of the pass where the shale comes sheer down to the edge of the loch – I believe the locality is pronounced Schloch'n ewer – a heavy squall was causing us to lose way and my flies must have sunk six or eight feet, when whir-r-r-r went my reel; the water parted close to the boat, and a great thick rosy brown fellow leapt three or four feet in to the air. I had just time to lower the point of my rod, ease the line, and so frustrate the obvious attempt on the part of the fish to break my fine trout cast by a slap of his great tail. Nichol had gained possession of my oar by this time, and was straining every sinew to hold the boat. Which way would he go? Thank goodness he was off downwind. Had he gone the other way Nichol could not have followed him; a few seconds' run would have exhausted my short line, and the first salmo-ferox that I had hooked in my life would at this moment have probably been enjoying life in the deep, dusky recesses of the weird and rocky pass, instead of undergoing a course of mummification in the garret of a taxidermist.

On he went, our friend steering an almost straight course for half or three-quarters of a mile ... I had only about one-fourth the requisite length of line on my reel, small flies, and correspondingly fine gut. I thanked my stars it was a fine-drawn four-yard cast, which had been specially made for me a fortnight before, and the soundness of which I had carefully tested. If I was severely handicapped in many points, I had at least the advantage of the services of one of the most experienced boatmen the countryside could produce. It was quite a treat to observe the dextrous manner in which he followed and seemed to anticipate the movements of our spotted antagonist.

On went the fish with never a check, utterly ignoring the two or three pounds of pressure I steadily maintained, the bit fairly between his teeth. Soon I found myself trying experiments based on the assumption that our spotted hero had stubbornly made up his mind to prevent me from having my way even in the smallest detail of the fight; hence, when we began to swerve slightly out of his straight course, I turned the point of my rod to that side, as if to assist him, when he would immediately change his mind and go the other way. Can I have been mistaken in this? I think not, for we enacted the game over and over again, until apparently our friend found the occupation of towing pall upon him, and he straightforward sounded and sulked.

Nichol held the boat while I pumped as strongly as I dared, but without result. My antagonist lay sullen and motionless, in the highest of dudgeons. After trying every means of civil persuasion in vain, and after expending every epithet in the vocabulary, both sacred and profane, and fairly driven to desperation, I ultimately decided to bombard the perverse brute with stones until I should succeed in dislodging him.

As we had been skirting the shore all the way, I told Nichol to edge the boat against the precipitous shore, only some five yards distant, where, without landing, we were able to gather a few large stones; then, pulling out again to windward of old brownie, we fired one missile after another. At the fourth discharge, his scaly majesty made a slight movement, then rushed forward like a boy discharged from school and nearly emptied my reel before Nichol could get into his wake; and, if we might judge from the pace, he had fairly gained his second wind. This time he made for the opposite shore obliquely downwind, but just before reaching it, made up his mind to return, and back we had to go.

All this time I had been huddled up in the bottom of the boat, so as not to make pulling harder than necessary by exposing my surface to the wind. Now for the first time, I took a hurried glance to see how Nichol was standing the strain, and when I saw his exhausted but game-to-the-last look I longed to give him a dram from my flask, though this was impossible under existing circumstances. Nichol seemed to read my thoughts, for he exclaimed 'dinna take your eyes off him. I'm doing fine!'

The mad rushes now ceased, and our good boat was steaming at half speed, with an occasional slow down. As if to favour us the wind lulled somewhat, and we could follow, when it was necessary, upwind. It must have been at the end of three-quarters of an hour that I first brought the quarry to the surface, when he came grudgingly, tugging and straining intermittently; but sight of us seemed to give him new life, which it took some ten minutes to exhaust. During a quiet interval I said 'Get the gaff handy, Nichol'. No answer.

'Nichol, have you got the gaff?'

Then he replied: 'No sir, we've left both gaff and net. I took everything out of the boat last night when I hauled her up out of reach of the waves, and must have forgotten to put them back. I remembered it the moment you hooked him, but I daren't tell you for fear it would upset you and spoil your hand, whereas if he broke away without your knowing the gaff was left behind I wouldn't have felt so bad.'

I must have ejaculated something, for Nichol said: 'Yes sir, that's just how I felt, but I gave it up, as I couldn't find words to do the subject justice.'

'What shall we do?' I asked.

'When he's not able to sit upright, we'll slip ashore, sir.' By this time the hardy warrior's strength was almost spent and as he came to the surface, lying on his side, the keen pleasure of seeing him almost ours was momentarily marred by observing him once more open his mouth and gasp heavily before he once more gave a sweep of his powerful tail and dived nearly to the bottom.

'Poor beggar, he's hard up. I almost thought I heard him sob that time he opened his mouth,' remarked Nichol, who, by this time, was edging towards the shore. The fish, having again surfaced was following quietly, lying on his side. Our difficulties were not yet ended, for the shale of the steep hillside afforded very insecure footing. I managed, however, to scramble up a few feet, and, reclining with my feet well buried among the loose stones, I began to wind up slowly.

'He'll come now, sir,' said Nichol, as he lay crouched at the water's edge. In he came, inch by inch, till he touched the stones.

Contact with them, however, seemed to infuse new life in to him, and I could not check his efforts, feeble as they were, though I put on all the pressure I dared. It looked like having to make a hasty run for the boat – no, he was turning; the strain that he scoffed at half an hour ago was too much for him now.

Lying on his handsome broad side, he allowed me to tow him gently towards Nichol who lay motionless. Almost before the stones were reached Nichol's right hand was buried under the great spotted gills, and the possessor of them was high and dry, struggling under Nichol's prostrate form. Neither would the latter move until I had put down my rod and passed a string through the still gasping gills.

'Don't take the fly out, sir,' said Nichol. 'Cut the gut and leave it in his mouth when you get him stuffed.'

Still embracing the fish, I followed holding the string, we scrambled back to the boat and laid out our trophy tenderly.

'Well, I've never seen a trout in grander condition, or finer marked,' said Nichol, as I poured out a good stiff dram …

'What is he – fifteen pounds?' I asked.

'More than that, sir. He's as near twenty as fifteen,' was the reply.

When the fish was cosily wrapped away in Nichol's oilskin in the prow of the boat, we rowed on to the river and landed at the little red shelter where luncheon was quickly disposed of and work recommenced, but neither minnow nor fly elicited any response, and at 5 pm we made for home.

Great were the rejoicings that night at Carron Lodge, and many a toast drunk. Nichol, getting the scales, said: 'You hold him up, sir, your arms are stronger than mine. Now, towards the right. Fifteen and a half pounds! But I had thought him more, and so he was when he first left the water. I'll pack him early tomorrow morning, and send him off from Taychreggan Hotel by the boat to the stuffers for you, sir.'

When pipes were finished and glasses emptied, candles were called for and I, for one, slept none the worse for my eighty minutes' exciting tussle. When shall I have such another?

By the outbreak of war in 1939, the age of the ferox tyros was over. Angling literature, even in peace, omitted giant brown trout from its coverage. Heroic tales of windswept lochs and wise old ghillies belonged to a previous era and the fishermen turned their attentions to other species; but great old stories survived between the musty pages of forgotten books.

Ricky and I sometimes wondered why the old masters did so well when their methods differed little from ours. History suggested that the Victorians and Edwardians may have had more ferox to fish for, but they had the idiosyncrasies of greenheart rods, silk lines and wooden star-back reels to contend with. We could only admire them and fish on, and find some comfort in another pearl of Colquhoun wisdom:

Sometimes, in spite of all the odds, the bungler gains the day.

31. The Fyrish Monument.

32. A last day pike.

29. A 7lb Irish ferox.

30. *Mayfly*, Patrick's boat.

27. Lunch on Canavar.

28. Galway: Gomorrah after Eden.

25. The mooring at Lal Faherty's place.

26. A ferox is hooked, Corrib, 2010.

23. The second morning on Corrib.

24. A 6lb ferox from Corrib.

21. Beneath the black water.

22. Setting out at Lal's bay.

19. Corrib from one of its many islands.

20. The deep water of Corrib.

17. Patrick at the helm.

18. An 11lb Corrib ferox.

15. Dawn on Lough Corrib, 2010.

16. The first morning on Corrib.

13. A brace of Loch Shin ferox.

14. Ricky finds them beneath the black water, 1999.

11. Loch Shin, 1997.

12. A 5lb ferox, Shin, 1999.

9. The stone circle at Kildermorie.

10. A Loch Cama brownie, 1998.

7. A Veyatie brownie, 1998.

8. A juvenile ferox trout, Loch Veyatie.

5. The Kildermorie shoreline.

6. Monsters at 124ft.

3. Ricky trolling at dusk.

4. Loch Shin brownies.

1. Bodle's Burn – the beginning of the story.

2. The first ferox trout, Loch Shin, 1997.

13

A HAMPSHIRE
DISTRACTION

The lake was big, 30 acres or more, dammed at its southern end and tapered to a point over a mile away in an extended isosceles triangle – a classic carp water. There was a boathouse, sunken islands, tangled neglected willows stooping into the margins and the musty smell of an ancient landscape. The grounds were private and the water belonged to old money, but fishing was permitted for a lucky few who knew who to ask.

The water carried a strange colour when I first saw it, a chalky pale green that never did quite disappear in the years that I fished there. Local experts blamed it on an algae bloom but it looked unnatural in every way. It was a strange place, the Bishop's Lake.

I had joined its syndicate with other members of the Golden Scale Club and it had become our opening night water, our first choice each June when the carp season began at midnight on the 15th. There were shoals of bright tench, a population of small 'wildie' carp between 5 and 10lb and, most desired by anglers, giant mirror and common carp rumoured to reach weights of 40lb and more.

It was these that we sought, with little success, but it didn't matter that few men ever caught them. A trek around the long east bank, through the woods towards the shallows, was akin to walking with Alice through the Looking Glass. There were caves and grottos and follies hidden among the undergrowth, sculpted verandas extending to the shore, a sunken arboretum and a charming, benevolent sense of oddness that was hard to shake. Whenever I heard footsteps behind me in the undergrowth, there was an even chance that it might be a curious doe, a bailiff or the Mad Hatter. Often it was fellow club member Ferneyhough, which amounted to much the same thing.

The Bishop's Lake became my favourite when I grew tired of the pool where Fat Keith swam. The carp at Bishop's were a mystery; they had been stocked centuries before, in all probability by monks, and nobody knew how many were there or how big they had grown. We could see vast shoals of them on some days but on others they would vanish. On quiet summer mornings a blue-backed monster could drift in front of you at any moment and render you speechless with its imperious bulk. Importantly, none of these fish had names. It wasn't ferox fishing, but it had an integrity all of its own.

There were rainbow trout in the lake, stocked in the fifties in a misguided attempt at fishery management, and we were anything but fond of them. Elsewhere they might have offered good sport to men with fly rods and gaudy lead-weighted lures, but in such a unique corner of England they were incongruous at best. At their worst, they were pests. They grazed like carp over our beds of sweetcorn and maggots, and many a quiet evening's float fishing would be violently interrupted by the arrival of a silver pirate in the swim. The fizzing bubbles would stop, tench would scarper and we would be left only with silver and crimson and a great deal of swearing.

Often, their tiny teeth cut our lines and they would fall off in a final act of ignominy, but when one came to hand it was invariably dispatched. Anna's cat had no qualms about eating American interlopers.

In the year that Anna and I went to Ireland, I heard about the brown trout in the Bishop's Lake. One of the fishermen mentioned them, casually, and he even referred to them as ferox. I spoke to Ferneyhough and he confirmed that they were there – not many of them, perhaps, but some.

Of course, there were no *salmo ferox* in the Bishop's Lake, not, at least, in any way that made sense to Ricky or me. The waters of southern England were not carved by glaciers and there were no mountains or arctic lakes when the ice receded. There were no charr, no bottomless gullies of cold Highland water where giant trout could skulk and grow. The climate owed more to mainland Europe than to the Scandinavian north, and always had. It was not ferox country. But, in its curious green waters and in the shadows of its follies, there were a few enormous brown trout.

Popular legend had it that these trout had worked their way up from the stream below the dam and had settled in the lake, and they had grown very large. Their presence was known only through sightings and, as far as I could ascertain, these had all been in the deeper water. Nobody knew very much about them. Nobody had fished for them, either, and I decided I should be the first.

I didn't know anybody who had ever gone ferox fishing on a tranquil English carp lake. I didn't know anybody who would want to, either, and was slightly embarrassed by the whole idea. I decided that my efforts should be covert. I told no one in the club about my plan and vowed only to reveal all when I had a trophy-sized fish to boast of. Their mocking would be all the more bearable when borne of jealousy.

Trolling was out. There was no boat, and even if I had managed to secure permission to use a vessel of some sort, I didn't have one of my own. Every effort would have to take place from the bank side and involve spinners or dead fish for bait. And so, from 16 June I began to keep a spinning rod and a box of lures in the boot of the old car. It was out of sight, and if discovered could be dismissed as detritus from my last trip north. When nobody was there, I would cast from the dam wall.

I chose small plugs and lures – Hornet Fire Tigers and Big S's which rattled and bobbed and sat at a reasonable depth. There was a great deal of weed to contend with in the summer and my lures had to search just above them, perhaps 5ft below the surface. It was late June before I got my first chance.

Ferneyhough was supposed to be there, but he was late. He was always late, and I knew that arriving on time would give me three hours of spinning before I would have to return to the car for a float rod and pretend to be a gentleman angler. I chose a spot half-way along the dam and, among the lilies and potamogeton beds, began to fish for giant brown trout.

The lures worked well, wobbling sub-surface and sending out pulses around them as I pulled them back in. In short order, I caught perch. Ten of them. None of them was longer than 8 inches and each of them inhaled the lure with rapacious hunger. And then the perch vanished, suddenly and inexplicably. I soon caught the cause of their departure, a pike of 7lb, from a lake that was reputed to have none. I took it down to the stream below the dam wall and released it into the water from where it had once come.

There were three other similar attempts that summer. On each of them I caught perch and pirates, but no more pike. My efforts went unnoticed by my friends and I was glad of that. Shortly before the summer holiday began I decided to have one last try – at night.

If there were brown trout in the lake, and I had seen none to confirm it to be so, I imagined that they would have fed on the silver fish, the roach and perch and fry of larger specimens. With this in mind I arrived at the Bishop's Lake with a bag of dead sprats from a Wiltshire fishmongers; it was a late July evening, balmy and still, and on the hour-long drive to the water I had felt both antici-pation and shame.

I would use three rods. This was one more than was allowed under syndicate rules, but nobody was there and one more rod couldn't add to my now considerable sense of guilt. The sprats were injected with air and fish oil to give them an extra scent and levitate them above the bottom weed. The shame took on serial killer proportions.

Nothing happened through the night. Fry flipped and skittered in front of me, a solitary carp rolled, but there were no ferox interruptions. This being the Bishop's Lake, I was never alone. Foxes scurried in the undergrowth and owls ghosted overhead. Bats jagged my lines as they dived and soared. There was no road noise, no human sounds at all, but there was never silence. As an angler, I have always found night to be a time of magic rather than terror, and I enjoyed myself. It helped that the little creatures that inhabited the grottos of the east bank – the Mollies – were known to be friendly. I had never seen one, but I had heard enough to believe they were there.

It was only as the first light of the day appeared behind me that one of the baits twitched. I held my breath and put the back of my hand beneath the line to feel for life, and life was there. Slowly, curls of monofilament were pulled from the reel and a run developed. I waited until the fish was steadily swimming away from me and then wound down and struck the cane carp rod over my left shoulder. Something pulled back.

Minutes later, it was safely in my net, but it was not the largest ferox trout to come from a Hampshire lake. It was not the smallest either. It was a 5lb common carp. Suitably chastened, I made coffee on the boot of the car and drank it walking up the east bank, among the statues, caves and grottos. Every step was accompanied by shafts of light through ancient trees and the heady aromas of the Hampshire countryside. The mist was lifting and a beautiful carp lake was emerging from it, and I knew that the biggest folly of them all was mine. I never did cast again for a Bishop's trout.

14

FISHING FOR FEROX

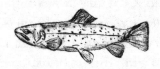

In the 1950s, London publisher Herbert Jenkins began issuing a series of short instructional books for fishermen. The *How to Catch Them* series was one of the most enduring in the sport and was still preaching its pocket-sized gospel in the 1970s when my brother and I began to fish. There was a book for each species of fish, as well as others that concentrated on the minutiae of the sport. *Tench, Pike, Barbel, Roach, Flatfish, The Fixed-Spool Reel, Gravel Pits* and *Artificial Flies* all made it into our collection at one time or another, but it was the carp edition, written by D.L. Steuart, which was the best loved and most dog-eared.

I met the author years later and told him so. He thanked me, but told me that the books were 'rushed off in a weekend, and the money was bloody rubbish'. It didn't change my opinions of the books, or of him. The series offered beautiful garish covers, clear illustrations and succinct advice, and all for the price of a few gob-stoppers. I loved them then, and still do.

Brown trout, rainbow trout, sea trout and brook trout all got the *How to Catch Them* treatment, but ferox never did. This was not surprising. By the fifties, *salmo ferox* had disappeared from the angling public's consciousness. The Victorian heroics of John Colquhoun were long forgotten and those who wanted gigantism could find it at one of the new stillwater trout fisheries, in the guise of pot-bellied, crimson-striped rainbows. These upstarts from the United States could be grown to ludicrous sizes in bathtubs and then released to sate the ambitions of the trout men. Elusive dinosaurs in the Highlands were just too much trouble and their book was never written.

Ricky had grown up with the same series and loved them, too. Sometimes, on long days in the boat, we joked about what a ferox edition might have said. *Go fishing in a loch. Start trolling. Use spinner or bait, it really doesn't matter. Expect nothing. When ten years have elapsed, give up and go and try for a rainbow. They really are frightfully accommodating.*

It would have been a very short book.

My fishing friends in Wiltshire might have agreed. Trolling was mindless and the hunt for ferox nothing more than a triumph of patience over good sense. To them, the method, if it could be dignified as such, involved little more than throwing a dead fish (or something cunningly designed to imitate one) behind a boat on a long line and dragging it around until something happened.

The Alness boys and I knew differently. Trolling for ferox proved far more exacting than we had ever expected it to be. There were considerable choices to be made each day and every one of them might condemn us to twelve hours of frustration and inactivity. Lures had to be chosen, depths agreed upon and trolling speed regulated. A single change to any of these would throw the others off-kilter, and it was at these moments that lines would tangle or reels would spontaneously combust.

Once these decisions had been taken, there were other perils to contend with. High winds could scupper a day before it had started, or confine us to a tiny corner of the loch where we might be several miles from the nearest ferox. When all was calm, there were thousands of acres to explore and the fish might be anywhere – or nowhere. Most calamitously of all, we could get everything right and still catch nothing. That happened a lot.

We chose our lures with something approaching scientific rigour. Silvers, blues, reds and browns were favourites, because they reminded us – and hopefully the ferox – of the small trout and charr they ate. Most were between 6 and 9 inches long, on the basis that the prey fish were of similar size. Particular preference was shown to those that were designed to dive to the depths, or which rattled and wobbled. When these failed to elicit a response, we would sometimes ignore science and play a wild card; there were lures in our boxes in colour combinations that hadn't been seen since Woodstock, and sometimes these psychedelic oddities worked. This was particularly evident at Loch Veyatie, where the juvenile ferox showed a preference for small pot-bellied plugs in yellow, lime green and black. These were called something like 'rattlin' hornet fire tigers', and came, not altogether surprisingly, from America. They defied all laws of science and good taste, but we used them all the same.

Less time was spent choosing appropriate rods. I liked using split-cane, and persevered with beautiful but wholly inappropriate Hardy salmon rods. Each of them took on an irreparable 'set' within a week, but as they were mercifully ignored by the fish it didn't seem to matter. Ricky was less troubled by aesthetics and knew better than to chase ferox with vintage bamboo. His rods of choice were weighty fibre-glass models designed for the sea. They were inexpensive and unfashionable, but close to indestructible. If a record ferox came along, my cousin had no intention of losing it to elaborately decorated panda food.

If rods were given little consideration, the choice of reels was equally unimportant. Ours were big, with strong clutches and the capacity to hold lots of line. Trolling involved no casting, and the reels themselves did little but sit in the holders waiting for the fish to arrive. Mine were vintage Abu Cardinals from Simon's shop, while Ricky's were chunky sea-fishing models from an Alness boot fair. They all worked equally well.

The most important item for trolling was the outboard motor. Victorian ferox men were obliged to row their boats – or rather, pay a small wiry man in tweed to do it for them – but the days of paying a few shillings to a hardy Highlander passed with the death of the old queen and none of our number were overly keen to take on this role. Ricky purchased a second-hand Yamaha engine which promised us a reliable 5hp, but Donian and his crew made do with an antiquated Seagull that belched, leaked and broke down with horrible frequency. It was noisy and left an oily wake wherever it went, but it was the best they could muster. Many long days ended with Donian or Stuart rowing back to the loch's edge, swearing with every pull of the oars, their lifeless prop hoisted from the water and silhouetted against a Highland sunset. To those of us on the shore, it could look almost beautiful.

When trolling proved unsuccessful, and this was often, we discussed trying for them in other ways. Stuart and Gordy were accomplished fly fishermen, Ricky too, and we knew that the ferox ran the rivers feeding the lochs in the autumn, spawning on the shallow gravels. We wondered whether they might be caught with a fly at these times, but never tried it. We also knew that the big trout sometimes fed nocturnally, when boats were forbidden to take to the lochs, and that they might be tempted with a static fish bait fished from the shore. This would involve poaching, which didn't worry us, and suffering the midges, which did. Some of the boys tried it, but Ricky and I chose not to join them.

He told me later that they had stayed several nights, drinking beer and smoking all manner of substances to frighten away the beasties. One small ferox came to the net, but their methods would never have got past the editors at Herbert Jenkins.

And so we kept on trolling and concluded that relentlessness was our finest weapon. The days were long, but that was no hardship. Ricky and I talked of fish, of family and of the landscape around us, and there were other days when we fell silent and just enjoyed being there. Every change in the weather was reflected in the colours of the mountains and the rhythm of the water beneath us, and we could not become bored. We experimented and explored, and eventually we caught.

By the time we did, we had realised that the joy was not in the capture but the simple pursuit. There was an unquantifiable sense of peace to be found in the repetition of the method and in the wilderness around us; a serenity in the process itself, but that was hardly the stuff of 1950s' fishing manuals. Neither Ricky nor I could claim to know how to catch the ferox trout, but we did know how to enjoy it.

15

BENEATH THE
BLACK WATER

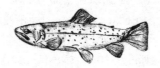

The second summer expedition began on a humid Sunday towards the end of August, but Anna was not part of it. She had opted to travel as far as the Lake District and to share a tent with me on the banks of Lake Coniston before returning home. Her career as a locum GP was going well and she would dispense wisdom and amoxicillin in Thatcham whilst I trolled endlessly on Shin. One of us had to earn some money, after all.

As we drove north into Cumbria, I was less than optimistic. Ricky had confirmed that the Highlands were experiencing an uncharacteristically languid summer and the fish were off the feed. He warned me that Loch Shin was 4ft lower than when I had last seen it and the ferox had seemingly disappeared to the depths to avoid heatstroke. On my cousin's advice, I added salmon and sea trout rods to the luggage. If the lochs were dead, we would go to the river.

Anna and I had fished many times since the coarse season had opened in Wiltshire. We had cast for carp and barbel and enjoyed lazy days on the Kennet and Avon canal where it ran through the village. The chub on the little River Loddon had proven especially susceptible to Anna's attentions and every passing hour offered an antidote to ferox fishing's do-or-die intensity. We caught some tiddlers and had a lot of fun.

Ricky, meanwhile, had been to Loch Awe with Stuart and Donian. The boys had spent four days in the land of giant ferox, but had conjured up only small pike and perch. They had met some of the Pitlochry gurus there, however, and their heads were now filled with new ideas. These included down-rigging, night trolling and fitting treble hooks to the tops of our lures because, in the words of one of the wise men, 'the ferox sometimes like to smash down on to the prey from above, and break their wee backbones'. If we needed reminding that we were fishing for a wild and savage creature, that singular fact was enough.

On the morning that we left the lakes, Anna and I enjoyed a few hours fishing on Esthwaite water. Both of us had sore heads from a riotous evening in Hawkshead and needed silence before our respective journeys. I fished with a fly, a gaudy white-and-silver lure called an Appetizer that was suggested by the bailiff, and Anna span with a tiny Mepps. The rainbow trout took to both with enthusiasm and we quickly caught six. By mid-morning the cerebral fog had cleared and we made for shore and said our farewells. I would miss her, but I needed to be in Scotland.

The A9 was quiet but for a north-westerly that gathered momentum as I reached Perth and stayed with me until Alness. It was still there on Monday morning and so Ricky announced that we would go to the river – Loch Shin could wait for calmer days.

My 10-year-old Peugeot burst with new equipment, some of it bought, but much of it borrowed from Ian, a fishing pal from home. Ian loved the southern rivers with their chub and barbel, but had weaknesses for the sea trout of West Wales and the salmon of the Highlands. This meant he had some fiendishly impressive rods and reels in his collection and, for reasons best known only to him, he was willing to lend them to me.

On Ricky's advice I had brought a double-handed salmon rod, a Sage 15-footer from Ian's collection, with which we would tackle the upper reaches of the Averon. In truth, it was too long for the intimate pools of the Novar beats, but Ian had assured me that it would offer control and distance and an ability to perform a tight roll-cast when trees got in the way. His advice was practical and technical and I nodded through the bits that I didn't understand, but I understood the sub-text; I was new at this and needed a rod which would do the hard work for me.

The Sage was worth more in monetary terms than the car which had taken me to Scotland, and when Ian handed it over he issued a warning, albeit with the polite understatement of a man raised in cultured circles: 'It's quite a decent bit of kit, and I really would rather it came back in one piece, or …'

He didn't finish the sentence, but I guessed that it ended with me being shot, excommunicated or set upon by his two gun dogs. They were called Lucy and Midge and were adorable, but I still wouldn't have fancied my chances.

I knew the final miles of the river quite well – the water that ran through Alness and poured out into the Cromarty Firth – having fished them as a boy with Ricky. The Douglas Pool with its high cliff and deep boiling water, the Sloosh with its ever-present salmon and oft-ignored 'No Fishing' sign, the Stick Pool with its concrete flood defences and long trough, and the Estuary beat where fly fishing gave way to any method lawlessness and where worming was king – each of these was dear to my brother and me, and even though we had rarely caught a fish in any of them, it was where Ricky had shown us how.

But, Ricky and Gordy were well connected with the local bailiffs and keepers, and with the best of the grilse run gone were able to bag three tickets for the Novar Estate, the costly private water that ran out of Kildermorie and belonged to the descendants of Hector Munro. If grilse were left in the river they would be resting in its deep pools and so the three of us bounced our way up the mountain road to the heavily forested estate. Later, in the silence of nightfall, we would realise that the Peugeot's exhaust hadn't survived the journey.

Ricky and I took the top of each beat, while Gordy jumped in below us. We followed the cast-step-cast etiquette of the river, working our way down each pool before retracing our steps with a new fly. When a pool was fished out or Ricky declared it empty of salmon, we moved to the next. By evening we had covered the Miller's Pool, the Yankee Tankee and the big corner pool of Beat 3, as well as every riffle and glide between them.

The rod proved to be excellent and before long the dark art of salmon-casting lost a little of its mystery. Spey casts and roll-casts invariably ended up slapping me across the face or depositing the fly in a tree, but a simple overhead cast was enough in most places. We used a variety of double-hook flies, Allie's Shrimps in shades of orange, red and black, and after lunch I tied on one of Ian's own, a Spicer Special. It was this creation that induced the only take of the day – a roll of silver, a brief snatch at the line and then nothing. We heard later that a solitary salmon had been caught on the 10 miles of the Averon that day and so our return – one missed fish and a small brown trout which hooked itself on a short line while I wrestled with a tangle – was deemed acceptable.

I knew from Ricky that salmon fishing could be like that. The big runs of fish on the Highland rivers had all but gone and there would always be days when nothing moved. The salmon fisher had to enjoy the process itself, the cast-step-cast repetition, the relentless pulse of the current on the backs of the legs, the whistle of the line as it shot forward and the new hope that came with every pool. My cousin and his pal both knew this and by the end of the day, so did I.

We gathered at nightfall by the car. There were blisters on my casting hand, line marks on my face and midgie bites on every conceivable surface of skin. My lower back ached from wading and my head thumped with dehydration, but I could at least call myself a salmon fisher – though not a catcher. Ian's ever-so-fancy rod had come through it all unscathed.

Gordy, Ricky and I barrelled back down the mountain in darkness, shouting over the roar of the punctured exhaust. Our day on the rarefied and fishless water of Novar had been tremendous fun, but we were more excited that the wind seemed to have dropped and we could return to Loch Shin. 'I'll tell yous boys,' Gordy said, 'after today, ferox fishing's gunna seem a piece o' piss.'

Our friend was wrong. The wind returned before dawn, and with it came rain, and lots of it. Ricky and I took a boat on Shin, Gordy and Donian another, and we fished the lower end of the loch for two days. On the first, we trolled small fire tigers over the shallow water of the loch's edge and took twelve brownies. Most were very small, though a couple were over a pound and had the darker, predatory demeanour of trout that were about to 'go ferox'. On the second, with the wind a little calmer, we trolled the depths in the hope of something more sizeable, and caught nothing. Once again, we struggled to sink our lines and get them down to the bottom where bigger fish had shown themselves on Donian's sounder.

There was another boat on Shin during the second day and we could tell from the sideways position of its drift that the occupant was fly fishing. For most of the morning we kept our distance, but later our trolling took us towards him and so we pulled in our long lines. Ricky slowed the engine and we offered greetings. The angler – an old boy fishing alone – was expertly landing a trout. He grinned back and held a thumb aloft; his day had evidently been more productive than ours.

We met him again at dusk, as we tied up our boats at the jetty. There was a plastic bag next to his rods and creel and it bulged with small dead trout. Ricky and I had no trophies to show and explained to him that we were after ferox; weeks could pass without a bite. He held up a hand as if to silence our excuses and said that he knew all about it.

'Aye, I remember it well,' he said. 'Did a fair bit o' it m'self when I was younger. Caught a fair few, too, once I knew where to look.' In the gloom, his eyes sparkled with mischief and he drew heavily on his smoke. The man was part-elf, part Clint Eastwood, and he smelled of peat and Old Holborn. 'So tell me boys … have y' found them yet?'

We said that we had not, although our sounder had shown that large fish could be found in the deep water. We told him that we had caught a couple, on Shin and Veyatie, but that sport had been pitifully slow and it was proving difficult to get our lures down among the fish.

'I'm no' surprised you're no' catching then boys,' our new friend replied. 'You need to fish the shallower water – nae more than forty feet, thirty is better. The big chaps aye live out in the deeps, but it's the shallows where they go to feed. Y' need to put your baits among the wee fish, that's all, and they're no' likely to be oot there.'

He pointed dismissively towards the middle of the loch, half a mile away – the very water we had spent that day and many others trolling without luck. 'I always fancied ma chances in the shadows by cliffs or rocks, where it's no' too deep but its dark. You'll find your ferox there, sure enough, beneath the black water.'

The old man waved as he left and we watched in silence as he climbed the path into the hills and disappeared. Curls of smoke from his roll-up lingered in the space he had left and there was a damp patch of earth where his bag of trout had been, so we knew we hadn't imagined him. The wind and the rain were still in our faces and the sun had finally set behind the peaks of Assynt. We were in darkness now, but I knew my cousin was smiling as broadly as I was.

We didn't get back to Loch Shin that summer and so couldn't search the old man's black water. The Peugeot's exhaust was booked in for repair at an Alness garage the next morning and by the time it was done we had missed our opportunity. Instead, Ricky and I spent the afternoon chasing rainbows at a newly opened commercial fishery outside the village. It was landscaped and organised and full of stocked fish which cruised the upper layers in a shameless display of boredom. Worse still, anglers were expected to pay by the hour. It was as challenging as casting into a bath tub and as mercenary as an Amsterdam brothel, and we quickly concluded that fishing for wild trout was much more fun than catching tame ones.

Friday brought wind and rain on the east coast and the prospect of high winds on Shin, but the forecast further west was a little more optimistic, so we drove across the Highlands once more. Veyatie's boat had already been claimed so we fished for the day on its smaller neighbour, Loch Cama.

Cama runs south-east to north-west, parallel with Veyatie and surrounded by the lochan-dotted hills of Assynt. The two are joined at their southern ends by the Abhainn Mor River, but though they share their waters, each has its own character. Veyatie is a long glacial scar, a slice of ancient blue between two mountains, while Cama is wider, a mile shorter, full of bays and intrigue.

We found our boat moored at Cama's southernmost tip, between Elphin and Ledmore Junction, and in the silence of a cemetery. The shallowest water was there, sheltered by small islands, but beyond was another 3 miles of deeper water in which we hoped we might find a ferox.

We knew from one of our old angling guides that big trout had been caught there in the first half of the century and that was enough to pique our curiosity. There were stories of 8lb fish – bigger than any we had caught – and one of these would have been enough to make our summer, but we also knew that every loch we visited held its secrets. The ferox of the remoter Highlands were so neglected by man that the presence of 20-pounders might go unnoticed for decades.

Gordy was with us and wanted to wander the banks with a fly rod. Ricky and I, however, took to the boat; it was our last chance of a big trout before I left for England and we set up the trolling gear with no thoughts for other methods. My cousin tied on the small fire tiger which had proven so effective with the 'baby ferox' of Veyatie and I opted for a more conventional ferox lure: a charr-like 18-gram Lukki in silver and blue.

The weather on the west coast was better than on the east, but not by much. We were forced to stay close to shore and troll the shallow water round Cama's islands, but this accorded with the old man's advice and so we didn't mind. My heavier lure snagged on sub-surface weed, while Ricky's skittered above it in the upper layers. I changed it for a lighter model but persisted with the colour scheme and was rewarded with a fish in the afternoon. It was no 8-pounder, but was unquestionably a ferox. At 15 inches in length it was large enough to give me a tussle before coming to the net and it continued its protests in the boat. When I slipped it back overboard, in the shadows of a wooded island, it kicked its tail in defiance and sprayed me with cold, black water.

Ricky landed ten brown trout during the day. Each was small and dark, dotted with the purples and reds of its early autumn colours. He returned every one of them; it was not a day for filling a carrier bag with dead bounty. It was not a day for monsters, either, just one for being afloat with my cousin and catching fish. And yet every time a rod hooped over, we thought of Cama's secrets.

By late afternoon the winds were up and even the sheltered waters around the islands were troubled. The rain refused to leave us, and the peaks of Suilven and Cul Mor were hidden by mist and drizzle. Sunset was four hours away and yet we were close to darkness. As we passed beyond an island I caught sight of Gordy, slowly making his way around the shore and casting into the wind on a short line. Our friend was just a grey silhouette against a rocky, heather-strewn backdrop, but I could see him hunkering down in his coat and tugging at his collar between casts and I knew that he was drenched. When he saw me waving, he beckoned us in.

Gordy's day had been a soggy one, but he had caught plenty of fish on teams of small wet flies and now he was ready for home. Ricky and I didn't protest. We loaded the car and climbed the road into the hills, agreeing that Cama's uncaught monsters would have to wait for another day and another year.

I left Alness for Wiltshire the following morning and had all weekend to find my way to Anna's. The rain followed me and I stopped three times to peer into rivers and inhale the last Scottish air of the year. In the afternoon I took a detour to Penrith and stopped in an old tackle shop which was known to serve coffee to anglers crossing the border. There, I browsed its racks of second-hand rods and found another Hardy to add to my unnecessarily large collection. There were boxes of old phantom minnows, too, the favourite lures of the Victorian ferox men, and I took them as well. Later, I skirted the eastern limits of the Lake District, the southern extremity of glacial ferox country. And then the mountains were gone, and the urban sprawl of England stretched out before me.

So too did another winter of wondering and questioning and analysing. A second season had passed since catching our first ferox trout and yet they mystified us still. We knew of dozens of lochs that held them and our techniques matched those used by every ferox guru from Colquhoun to Greer – but we couldn't catch them. The old boy's wisdom gave us hope for the following season, but eight months would pass before we could cast for them again. As I drove the final miles to Anna's house, I rang my cousin.

'We'll get them next year,' I promised.

'Aye, maybe. I hope you're right,' he replied.

For once, I was.

PART III: 1999–2010

16

NORTHERN SOUL

The Alness boys who joined us in our ferox hunt were as much a part of Ricky's life as the lochs, the river and the village itself. They were the pals he had known all his life, through school and work, and the darker days when there were no jobs to be had. My brother and I had often met them on our childhood holidays – smoking outside the chip shop, gathering at the bottom of Coulhill or lining up to take their turn at the Stick Pool's salmon. We were very young and they doubtless found us irritating, but we were Ricky's cousins and so they treated us well. Whenever they fished, we were allowed to tag along.

Each of them was an expert with a fly rod and had a deep empathy with the river. They fished because it was what boys in the village did and they did it well, but they were also willing to abandon all ethics and poach a salmon when the hotels and restaurants were paying well. The method required a length of thick orange twine, lead weights and a huge treble hook, and was known to locals as 'ripping'. It was bloody and unsporting and could take the skin off your knuckles if the fish was big. Nobody liked it, but there were times when it was the only way to make some money.

When the river was too low, or the salmon weren't running, the boys went to the lochs of Easter Ross and Cromarty. They camped and fished at Kildermorie and Dalnacloich, and some of my finest memories are of the times when Chris and I were allowed to join them. At Dalnacloich, especially, it was never clear whether or not we had permission to be there, but the Alness boys told us they would speak to the bailiff and 'take care of it'. They were fearless, and their bravery became ours, too – until the midgies arrived, when we would all blow smoke and hide beneath our anoraks and secretly wish it was time to go home.

It was one of the Alness boys who gave Chris and I our first cigarettes; another who plucked a bottle of home-distilled whisky from a cave by the river and urged us to try it. We were 10 or 11 at the time and they were just a few years older. Back home we might have reported such tearaways to the police or headmaster, but on the boulder-strewn banks of the Averon their lawlessness was not a threat to us but a life-enhancing addition to a holiday with Ricky. Even if my brother and I could barely throw a fly line, we could at least spit the remains of our roll-ups into the foam and declare, 'it's pish, boys, they're no' havin' it tonight', and we could feel like men.

The boys taught us other words and phrases that would help us throughout our lives – words for describing small fish, very big fish, policemen, unattractive girls who stood outside the chippy every night and lads who preferred playing with dolls to being by the river (none of us knew any of the latter, but we had heard rumours of them and they merited several names). The boys were smart enough to tell us to keep our new vocabulary to the river and never use those words in front of our ma. She had grown up with their mothers and knew them still, and in the small universe of the village a cuff round the ear could be hastily arranged.

Like Ricky, the Alness boys had the river's dark waters running through their veins, and its viral presence continued past boyhood. They fished whenever they could, abandoning jobs if the spring run was an especially good one and happily forgoing luxuries to fund each adventure. When they became men, every employer and every girl had to accept that fishing was just what they did.

I knew Gordy best of all, and when the ferox hunt began he was there to sweep the net under the first fish. Gordy was quiet, thoughtful, an outdoorsman with the efficient, wiry frame of someone who laboured hard in all weathers for his money. He tried spells of conventional work at the distillery, but these inevitably ended when the salmon started running and he felt compelled to walk out. Gordy was not a man to be kept caged in a factory or office, and eventually he succumbed to the pull of the rivers and mountains and became a gamekeeper. The work was seasonal and unreliable, but when it came up it suited him – he would have been there anyway.

Work was never easy to find in Alness, but for those willing to graft long for honest wages, it could sometimes be had. In Baldy's time it was among the hydroelectric projects in the hills, but in Ricky's it came with the boom in North Sea oil. When the rigs were towed in for repair at Nigg, there was good money to be earned and the boys knew this. Several became welders, including Stuart and the brothers I knew as Bisto and Popper. Donald Ian, who we all knew as Donian, was a marine for a time but later joined his pals.

Whether there was work about or not, all of them found time to be by the river and to travel with us to Shin and join in the great ferox hunt. We went there as equals. By the time *salmo ferox* swam into our heads, I was no longer Ricky's wee cousin, a noisy upstart to lead astray – they had taken care of that job a long time ago and they had done it rather well.

There were unspoken arrangements whenever we went to Shin and these never varied. Ricky and I took a boat together, with my cousin in charge of the outboard. Gordy joined us when work allowed and he and I would then share the two outer rods. A second boat would be used if Stuart and Donian came along and they too could accommodate a third angler if one of the other boys was free to fish that day.

I was happy with this. My motives in heading north each year had always been blurred, but I knew that time spent with Ricky was as precious as the fishing itself. My role in the ferox hunt was different to that of the boys; for them, it was all about the trout. The boys fished most days on the river or one of the local lochs and so ferox were an enthralling variance on something that they did all the time. They lived and worked in the landscape and were less inclined to become poetic about it. Each of them was smart enough to know that they were lucky, but they also asked enviously about life in munificent England, which was as distant and intriguing to them as the big skies of Sutherland were to me.

But my ferox hunt was different. I wanted to catch the fish, but I also wanted to sit in a boat with Ricky and feel part of a family I had all but ignored for a decade. I knew from my mother about our shared histories – about the Sinclairs and the Douglases, the Frasers and the Crockets – but it was only with my cousin, on the waters of the lochs, that it began to feel real. Going fishing with Ricky was about reclaiming an idyllic childhood and placing myself in a landscape that was foreign to me, but to which I felt drawn. Sooner or later I knew I would have to find some equilibrium in England, but for now there were questions to be addressed in the Highlands, and these could only be answered in the company of Ricky and his pals. There were some fish to be caught, too.

17

HERE IS A SUNRISE

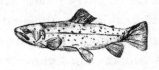

I had promised Ricky that the third year of our ferox hunt would be successful and when winter passed and May arrived, I still believed it would be. This confidence did not come from any significant improvement in our knowledge or techniques, because we were doing much the same as we always had. It came from the wise words of the old man we had met at Shin, and from a silent mantra known to all fishermen: *if you keep doing it for long enough, something will happen.* By the beginning of our third season, we had spent enough time afloat to believe that our time had finally come.

It had been a curious winter. Anna and I had parted in September, spectacularly and acrimoniously. My obsession with ferox trout – and by then I had accepted it as such – was not entirely to blame. The insults exchanged across the bar and over the telephone during that tempestuous autumn rarely mentioned them, but we both knew that my dreams were very different to hers and my heart was in the Highlands. Later, when the frosts arrived and the pike began to bite, Anna and I reconciled as friends and accepted that we were better as such and it would always be so. I moved in with my parents, caught a few fish at weekends and began playing bass in a local pub band. I also turned 30, and tried not to think about the things I had failed to achieve in that time.

When spring became early summer, it was time to head north once more, and now I would be doing it alone. I loved the journey itself; the solitude was comforting after the hurly-burly of the classroom and the far more infantile squabbling of the staff room. In that third year, a long, silent road stretched in front of me and at last it felt like the wild frontier that Polly and I had sought. At its end, I was sure, was a loch full of ferox trout.

The old Peugeot would take me there. It was a basic model with a small engine and its cassette player had jammed. I could play the tape that was stuck inside it – in fact, it played all the time, whether I wanted it to or not – but I could not change it. Thankfully, the eject mechanism had died when one of my choices, rather than one of Anna's, had been playing, and the album in question was entirely appropriate for the road to Alness. Teenage Fanclub's *Songs from Northern Britain* was a jangling paean to the Highlands and looped endlessly on the broken machine. Whenever I needed noise, I only had to turn up the volume and the sounds of Scotland, albeit interpreted through surf harmonies and vintage Fenders, filled the car.

I left Wiltshire in the evening, as the sun disappeared behind the Vale of White Horse. An hour later, the car dropped down into the valley at Birdlip, beyond the old Air Balloon pub, and the lights of Stroud and the M5 stretched across the horizon. I glanced right, to the single-track lane that marked a world where Laurie Lee drank cider with the eponymous Rosie. I remembered that perfect seduction and the O Level that had brought it to me, and then I accelerated. Messing about with girls hadn't done either of us much good. Lee had abandoned the Cotswolds for Civil War Spain, and I was fleeing to Scotland.

I counted off the M5, and then the M6, in rivers. The roads themselves were flat and featureless until the north was reached, and the night traffic largely juggernauts. There was little to see but the grim skeletal outline of industrial England, silhouetted against a light-polluted sky around Birmingham, Stoke-on-Trent and

Manchester. In daylight I might have enjoyed watching the landscape undulate and change and wondered at the story of England's
imperious emergence, but at night there were only the signs for
the rivers and the blackness running below them. I drove over the
larger, known waters with little interest – the Severn, Avon, Dane
and Ribble held no magic for me. The smaller brooks and streams
intrigued me more, particularly those with no grand motorway
signs or fishing reputations; the Swilgate, the Tirle and Doxey
brooks, the Salwarpe, the Staffordshire Tame and then, after three
hours' driving, Lancashire's River Douglas. I knew that some
would be dried up or canalised, but others would have pools of
quiet water where uncaught trout might grow to stupendous size.

Small streams like these always appealed to me. When my brother
and I were very young, we used to swim and fish (as poachers, of
course) in the little River Meon in Hampshire, in the water next to
the Fisherman's Rest overlooked by the ruins of Titchfield Abbey.
It was close to home and to school and with our pals we built rope
swings and ignored the signs that told us we were on private land.
We knew that the fishing was reserved for an exclusive syndicate
of grown-ups, but we also knew that we could run faster than
any of them. None of us ever caught anything there, apart from
minnows; it was a clear chalk stream and we were usually there in
the heat of August. Furthermore, we didn't know the difference
between a Greenwell's Glory and a feather duster, so our chances
were slim. Every fish we saw darted into invisibility the moment
we stood up to cast our worms at them. The Meon taught us that
trout were fiendishly clever, lightning quick and usually very small.
It also taught us that tiny streams could hold surprises, because one
or two of those fish we glimpsed were huge.

It was late now and my mind began to wander. I considered the
fact that not every giant trout was a ferox, but every ferox was a
giant trout. To catch one, man needed to think like a scientist and a
hunter. Once caught, the same trout turned man into a poet. How
many troubled men would be at peace if trout didn't exist at all?
And was a big trout from a stream more of a monster than one the

same size from a huge loch? What if a trout moved between loch and river? Plenty did …

The reflectors of the central reservation began to fuse with my own headlights. It was time to open some windows and turn up the volume.

> Sky is forever clear
> Roads never made it here
> Forests are deep and green
> Like nothing we've ever seen …

Every river crossed told me I was closer to Scotland, but the Douglas was the first whose name suggested it, too. Others followed – the Yarrow, Brock, Calder and Wyre. Each would have been a special place to its anglers, but I ignored their promise and pressed on, stopping for petrol in Lancaster. The Peugeot's tired engine chugged relentlessly on, over the delightful Lune, with its famed runs of salmon and sea trout, and towards the tarns and becks of the Lake District and beyond.

I couldn't see the change in the landscape, but I could sense it. Stars vanished behind invisible mountains and the ground lighting softened and was gone. The sky and its horizon felt bigger and wilder, though I couldn't say why, and the motorway which had felt so integral to the fabric of the English midlands now felt incongruous. I blinked furiously and gripped the steering wheel tightly, promising myself a break when the final miles of England were behind me.

In the early hours, I crossed the border and stopped for coffee at Gretna. I had a small stove and a canteen of water and brewed up in the quiet of a lay-by. The A74 was almost silent, the sky clear and windless, so I jumped and stretched and sang unashamedly, and waited for track 5 to come around.

> We're going over the country
> And in to the Highlands

To look for a home
We're leaving nothing behind us,
And no-one will find us
When we're on our own.

The best of the journey was still to come, and would happen as the sun rose.

The A74(M) took me as far as Glasgow's eastern fringes and I recalled the night when my father had driven us through its centre on a wayward journey home from Ricky's. It had been in the late 1970s, long before an ambitious makeover had brought it 'city of culture' status, and we had been in search of an open petrol station. The tenements, winos and smackheads were still there, and the reputation of the Gorbals lingered. I remembered dad telling us, in a sombre tone that he rarely used, to lock the doors of the Austin Maxi.

I also remembered the girl I had dated, briefly, when I had started college. Julie dressed smartly and worked at the bank, while I devoured European History and hung with a bohemian crowd; but in all other respects she was far more worldy than I. It was Julie who led me to the hayloft for my own first cider – and after only a week. And then she went to Glasgow to see her cousins for a few days, and met a boy who looked like the singer from Wet Wet Wet. She didn't come back, and my feelings towards bank staff and Glasgow and insipid pop-soul never did recover.

I skirted the city limits before heading north-east, crossing Scotland at its narrowest point towards Stirling and then Dunblane. I was back for a short time in a world of artificial lights and urban development, but soon joined the A9 to Perth, knowing that the last hours would be spent in the mountains. Dawn was approaching and all was perfect.

I had reached ferox country. This was how the Alness boys and I thought of the land around Pitlochry. Anglers throughout the country knew it for the quality of its salmon fishing, and that it was where three rivers met, but for us it was the home of the gurus and their research facility. It was also close to some of the great ferox lochs of the Victorian past and of the future. To the west were Lochs Tay, Tummel, Garry and Rannoch, and each was immortalised in the writings of old men and in the deeds of Greer and his pals. They could not be seen from the road, but I knew they were there, among the mountains and forestry of Tay Forest Park. I stared into the foaming water of the Tummel, which snaked west to Rannoch Moor, to a bleaker landscape where wolves once roamed. I promised myself that I would fish its waters one day.

The A9 swung gently north-west towards Glen Garry, and I silently raised my cap to Ron Greer. It was here that he began a campaign to return indigenous trees to the highland slopes, hitching round the mountains in 1974 with young saplings on his back. His motives were good; as a biologist, angler and conservationist, he knew that the beautiful glacial-scarred slopes and sheep-dotted mountains were fine for selling tins of shortbread and other tourist tartanry, but the view loved by visitors was fraudulent and only a deciduous woodland environment would support the food chain of the region. Greer won local and national awards, and by 1990 had been joined by many others who knew his logic to be sound. The Loch Garry Tree Group grew from the ideas and hot-headedness of a young ferox tyro into a vital and brilliant conservation movement. From the silent cabin of the Peugeot, I thanked him.

It was 7 a.m. and I had been on the road for ten hours. I stopped for coffee once more, in a lay-by in the Grampian Mountains. The Cairngorms reached into a clear blue sky in the east, the Monadhliath Mountains hid the Great Glen and Loch Ness to the west, and I knew I would be with Ricky in little more than an hour. The early morning light was soft, all warm oranges and yellows. I turned up the volume one more time and it was track 2, my favourite.

'Here is a sunrise,' they sang. 'Ain't that enough?'

At that moment it was.

18

THE TROUT OF LOCH SHIN

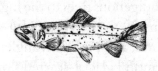

Ricky was waiting for me with a mug of coffee when I arrived in Alness. I needed to sleep, but my cousin had news. He and the boys had been fishing on Loch Shin at least once every week since mid-April and finally, in the shadows below the cliffs, they had found the ferox, just as the old man had said they would.

The season had started slowly after a bitterly cold winter and the water in Shin had taken an age to warm up. The loch had been unwelcoming, the small trout inactive and the boys' early outings had proven unsuccessful. But, by the end of April, the upper layers had benefited from extended periods of sunlight and big predatory trout had begun to move into the shallows and hunt the prey fish – and the Alness boys had been there waiting for them.

Ricky had a photograph to show me. It was under-exposed and blurred and was evidently taken at night with a cheap camera, but the five ferox trout on the grass next to my cousin were unmistakable. The smallest was perhaps 2lb, the largest nearly 7, and Ricky's grin spoke of bemusement, triumph and exhaustion.

'Ah thought I'd wait 'til y' got here before I said anythin'', Ricky said. 'Ye'd only have driven like an idiot and killed yer'sel'.' He was right.

The catch had been shared with Stuart and Donian, and was the best among several successful days. Between them they had landed more than a dozen ferox trout in May, all from Loch Shin and on a variety of spoons, plugs and fire tigers. Every one of them had come in 30–40ft of water, and the boys had reached the conclusion that the choice of lure was of far less importance than fishing in the right place and at the right depth. Their biggest fish so far had weighed 7½lb, but Ricky was confident that a double-figure fish was quite possible if they persevered. I was sure he was right about that, too.

The boys had formed the view that there were three generations of ferox trout in Loch Shin. There were the smaller fish of 1–2lb, immature ferox that had yet to develop fully the dark colours and enlarged jaws of their older kin. Then there were the adult fish, of 5–7lb, the lean predatory trout with kyped jaws and black flanks, of which there were far fewer. Finally, the boys believed there to be a third generation of fish, older and much bigger than any we had caught. These could weigh anything from 10–30lb and the boys had no evidence of their existence other than anglers' intuition and a deep, unproven faith.

We began on Shin the next morning and fished it for four long days. The wind was persistent but not prohibitive so we were able to explore the deeper northern shoreline, the water around the salmon cages and the dam wall. Rain was in the air all week, but it was the kind of drizzle that invariably comes with a grey Highland sky and we didn't mind. Ricky fished with the fire tigers that had served him so well, and I used 4-inch spoons in trout and charr colours. We both fished with 4ft nylon traces, half-moon-shaped anti-kink vanes, cigar-shaped barrel leads of 2oz and a couple of ball-bearing swivels on our lines – this was the magic combination that we and the Alness boys had finally arrived at, and it worked. We caught some ferox trout and, in the end, we caught them easily.

On the first day we landed several brownies up to a pound in weight. The biggest were unquestionably predatory fish, but they were not yet the mature ferox we sought. We unhooked each of them in the water and returned them as gently as we could. On the second day, three 2-pounders and several smaller fish came to the net. All were taken by the salmon cages and regurgitated hapless parr in our nets. We decided to cross to the opposite shore for the remaining days and troll the black water north-west of Lairg in the hope of something bigger.

On the third day the loch was quiet and we caught only small brown trout, but Ricky was unconcerned by this and said that the big fish were sure to feed soon. And then, on the fourth day, we caught two good ferox trout, of 4½ and 5¼lb, in the shadow of a sheer cliff face on the northern shore. They came within minutes of each other.

They were not huge specimens but they were big enough for us, and were the fish we had waited three summers to catch. Ricky and I shook hands and took some photographs and beached to make coffee. There was very little to say, but Ricky said it all the same.

'About fuckin' time, mate.'

We laughed and shook hands once more, and then we silently put away our gear and chugged back to the angling club. It was late afternoon and conditions were fine, but we both knew it was time to go home. I threw a lure out on the way back, but the moment was over and the loch was silent once more.

We drove out of Lairg and through Invershin towards the Dornoch Firth. The Bonar Bridge took us into Easter Ross and we passed the Electric Hill and the turning for Sween Macdonald's. We were in the mountains now, 200 metres above sea level but still beneath the peaks of Struie and Cnoc an t-Sabhail and Bien T'uinn. Roadside posts stood ready to mark off the snow drifts that would arrive in winter, but for now the forecast was fair and summer lay ahead. After 15 miles the road dropped down towards the Cromarty Firth and we were back in Alness. Fyrish stood proud in the west and the main street bustled with life. Kids cycled or ran with chip suppers in their hands, a man sat in the bus shelter with a can of Tartan clutched to his belly, and the river flowed through the heart of the village, as it always had.

I didn't know it then, but many years would pass before I would next cast for the trout of Sutherland. When summer came I knew it was time for a change.

I didn't go north to Ricky in August, as I had in previous years. Instead, I flew to Atlanta, hired a Chevrolet and drove it around Georgia and Tennessee. I bought a bass guitar in Knoxville and took the opportunity to get drunk in Memphis and Nashville and sleep in cheap motels. I marvelled at the wide roads and big skies, the red hills where the crosses still burned on summer nights, and the dusty towns where uptown meant white and downtown meant black. It was like nothing I had seen before and I didn't think about ferox trout at all.

Back in England, the band I had joined was getting more attention than it deserved. We were a pub covers outfit, a noisy good-time racket with little style and even less substance, but we were getting bookings. We played at Al's and Roo got up and sang a raucous version of Abba's *Waterloo*. Anna came to see us on the same night and brought her new man with her, and it felt like we had all moved on. I didn't mention Scotland or ferox trout, and nor did they.

Sutherland seemed further away with every day, until I could no longer bring to mind the cliffs at Shin or the peaks of Suilven, although I thought about the boys and the fish from time to time. The Highlands and the Frasers were part of me once more, but ultimately, as is the way with all fishermen, I was left only with memories and a handful of photographs.

The Alness boys fished on, and so did Ricky. My cousin rang me whenever another fish came to their boat and, in October, sent me a clipping from the *Scottish Daily Record*. There was a suitably crass tabloid headline, 'Ricky's leader of the pack', and above it a photograph taken in his Alness backyard. Ricky was all dressed up in tweed and deerstalker and in his left hand was an enormous ferox trout. The article was brief, but impressive:

Ricky Fraser's years of trying to catch a specimen brown trout paid off with this beauty during a recent expedition on Sutherland's

Loch Shin. The huge trout tipped the scales at 18lb 4oz and was caught trolling. Ricky's ambition is to connect with a Scottish record brownie, but in the meantime he's achieved another ambition by winning the Daily Record/Daiwa Fish of the Week prize.

By winter, I had become a little bored of thundering my way through *Hit me with your rhythm stick* for the drinkers of Wiltshire. I needed to go fishing again, and the return of my brother from the Middle East was timely. Chris had spent two years among the sailfish of Abu Dhabi and wanted to catch barbel and pike, so we did just that. The Kennet in Berkshire was experiencing an unexpected renaissance and its barbel population was attracting anglers from all over the country. We joined clubs that rented the water between Thatcham and Reading and we caught plenty.

Barbel fishing was so different from trolling in the Highlands. The techniques were straightforward – legering or float-fishing with maggots or small pieces of luncheon meat was enough to conjure a few bites – and an evening wandering the pastoral banks of the river with net, rod and creel was edifying in itself. Importantly, we could expect to catch three or four fish before sunset.

It was the first time that Chris and I had fished together since the summer of our O Levels, but it was as if nothing had changed. He was now married and had a son and I was an overly cynical teacher with large debts and a romantic past best described as 'complicated', but down by the river we were children once more.

Within months, Chris announced that he and his family were moving to North Lincolnshire. Soon after, he rang to say that he and a friend had secured the fishing rights on an old estate lake, a quiet lily-fringed pool designed by Capability Brown which had not been fished in forty years. There were rumours of big pike and I was invited to join in the adventure.

Our first day together by the secret pool was remarkable. We fished simply with pike bungs and deadbaits and we all caught monsters. My float disappeared four times and the fish I landed were all between 18 and 21lb. Chris caught a 23-pounder while Roger, his friend, caught a giant of 32lb. The pike were savage and brightly marked, and reminded me of the predatory trout of Sutherland.

We enjoyed a golden winter and caught many more of them.

Ricky was pike fishing on the lochs of Cromarty and landing a few of his own. Scottish law decreed that the trout were to be left alone between mid-October and March but pike, as a fish of the lower orders, were afforded no such protection and gave the anglers of the Highlands something to cast for in the winter months. Stuart, Gordy and Donian were with Ricky and had invested in tents, stoves and other comforts. I smiled when I heard about this; when the boys undertook a project, they invariably did it with conviction. Ricky and I spoke every few weeks to compare catches, and even though I wasn't there with them, it felt as if we were sharing an adventure of sorts.

In the following spring Ricky called to tell me that Donian had caught a 15lb ferox trout from Shin, on a day out with Stuart. The old Seagull engine had held up and a mighty fish had taken a liking for one of Donian's outsized lures. Ricky and the boys were joyous and so, from a distance, was I.

We didn't know it then, but it was the last big ferox the boys were to catch; the east coast salmon runs were improving and there were big fish to be caught in the river that ran through the village. There was magic to be found in the home waters of Alness and the boys were too canny to miss out. And so they returned to the Stick Pool, the Estuary, the Douglas Pool and the Sloosh, and cast their flies on the river where they were kings. If the grilse or the spring-ers failed to show, and there would always be days when the river was empty, the boys went to the smaller lochs around Cromarty, just as they had when Chris and I were boys.

Not too long after the capture of his monster, Donian and a pal drove north-west in search of wild trout and adventure in the wilderness of Durness. It was planned as a short trip, just a day or so among the limestone lochs where the brownies rose freely and grew very big, but they never made it there. It was early morning and the boys had been carousing the night before, and their car span out of control.

Donald Ian Sinclair died on a quiet Highland road on the way to a loch full of trout, just as the sun was rising.

19

FREDDY

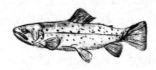

'Ten pounds an inch,' said the man with the long hair and the ear-
ring. 'Plus materials. You'll get change out of £300. Maybe four.
You don't even have to pay up front.'

It was 2006, the first weekend of the summer holidays, and I was
at the CLA Game Fair on the Broadlands Estate in Hampshire.
The man in question was called Trevor and I knew him, though
not especially well at that moment. We had met at a few events in
previous years and shared an interest in old rods and the barbel of
the Kennet and St Patrick's Stream. But we weren't talking about
barbel that day. We were talking about ferox trout – and one ferox
trout in particular.

I was there under false pretences, trying to be helpful on Ed the
Rod-maker's stand. He was there, legitimately, to sell his exquisite
rods. My role was to fetch the drinks and tubs of olives. In truth,
I was doing little to earn my ticket other than loitering and getting pleasantly disorientated on Pimms, but it was a sunny afternoon
and we were having fun. Trevor was our neighbour that weekend
and on his allocated stall were rows of wooden fish carvings. There
were barbel, perch, gudgeon and tench, all chiselled and whittled

and hand-painted by Trevor. They were beautiful, and reminded me of Ricky's story of the Kildermorie trout. Unwisely, I pulled out a picture of my first ferox, the Shin fish, and Trevor suggested that a life-size carving would make a spectacular addition to my tackle den.

'She'll love it,' he said. 'And if she doesn't, don't worry. It's your den.'

'She' was my wife. I had married in haste in 2001, walking up the aisle with a girl who had sung occasionally with the band. It had seemed like the proper, grown-up thing to do; I had just ascended to the school's senior management team and I now wore suits and shirts that required cuff links. I had retired from pub rock and wild trout chases – a pretty wife and a mortgage were part of the new, twenty-first-century plan.

She was a regular at Al's and a friend to Anna and Roo. We had run with the same crowd for many years but that would not be enough to hold us together. Within four years both of us knew that our union survived only through loyalty and stubbornness. By the time of the Game Fair weekend I was sleeping in the spare room and we were communicating through post-its on the refrigerator door.

Cat food, your turn.

Pay the bloody phone bill, I paid last time.

Going fishing, back eventually.

It had all started quite well, with a visit to Ricky. Before we married, I took her to the Highlands for a short break in the hope that, by some sort of geographic osmosis, my new fiancée would understand the hold the mountains and lochs had over me. In reality we wandered round the Loch Ness museum in Drumnadrochit and the homogenous shops of Inverness, and Ricky and I talked about fish in the evenings. I barely cast a line all week, but I was in the heady, selfless first moments of a romance and it didn't feel necessary.

She didn't want to go back to Scotland after that – too cold, clothes shops too ordinary, too far away – and so I didn't return for a long time, either. When I pulled the ferox picture from my wallet and handed it to Trevor, I hadn't seen Ricky or a Highland loch for five years.

Trevor was keen to carve a ferox trout. The colours were unlike any he had painted before, and he was impressed with the size of the creature. Trevor, as a barbel man who stalked the rivers and streams of Berkshire, thought of trout as small fly-supping irritants who were just a little too fond of the baits he cast for old whiskers. But when they were close to 2ft long, even he was interested. Especially at £10 an inch.

And so I left the photograph with Trevor that weekend, and he used the old cane carp rod in the picture to calculate the fish's dimensions. I told him not to rush it; the usual waiting time was up to a year, but it didn't matter if he took longer. I had to save up, after all.

Money was an issue. I had been in debt before the monster trout hunt had begun and so each trip had been funded by increased borrowing – first from the bank and later from a private firm in Swindon when the good people of Lloyds lost patience with me. Their interest rates would have made the most hardened member of the Cosa Nostra blush and I began the new millennium almost £20,000 in the red. Worse still, I was 31 years old with nowhere to live but my parents' spare room. But every time I looked at the photographs from Shin and Veyatie, I knew it had been worth it.

In the years after the abandonment of our Highland adventure, my finances became more stable but the recovery was partial; I had taken on a mortgage which had swallowed up previous loans but there was no equity in the house and now every prospect of a divorce to pay for in the future. I certainly couldn't afford to spend hundreds of pounds on a wooden ferox trout; the real ones had been costly enough. But it didn't stop me.

I got to know Trevor better over the next eighteen months. He called from time to time, to agree the wording for the board on which the fish would be mounted and to request further photographs so that he could get the colours *just so*. We visited stretches of the Kennet and the Holy Brook near his Reading home and talked about barbel. We talked about guitars and bands, too, and I learnt that Trevor was a talented musician with his own stories to tell. We met at game fairs and other gatherings, and at each he would assure me that the ferox was 'coming on rather nicely'.

The same could not be said for my marriage. We had yet to consult solicitors, but in all respects the relationship was over. I retreated to the attic of our little house with my books and rods, and with a sense of bewilderment about how life had led me to an unhappy corner of Swindon with a girl who found me wholly resistible. Even the post-it notes had stopped.

In the spring of 2008 Trevor called to tell me that the fish was ready and so I drove to Reading with a pocketful of cash; I found my way to a house that burst with rods and guitars and Marshall 4x12 cabs. There was a PA system behind the sofa, a newly restored Wallis Wizard drying in the kitchen and countless fish carvings in varying states of completion. A 4ft plank on the stairs was waiting to be turned into a 30lb pike. In the middle of this chaos, Trevor and the ferox were waiting.

The finished carving was remarkable. Its sculptor had been meticulous with every dark scale, with the black and gold patina of its gill covers and the primitive kype of its jaw. Every ray of its broad tail and pectoral fins spoke of the power and ferocity we had encountered on Shin more than ten years earlier. It was perfect.

I took it back to my Swindon attic and, in an act of unnecessary anthropomorphism, named it Freddy. Months later, the two of us left the house and did not return. A long period of acrimony and litigious squabbling was about to begin, but my exquisitely carved friend and I were ready for it. We were in a new wilderness, and the skies were wide open once more.

20

WINDERMERE

If marital calamity had an upside, it was the gift of time. Suddenly I had lots of it, and a new opportunity to fritter it away came along soon enough. A publisher friend took pity on me and gave me something to do, and for much of 2009 I travelled around Britain gathering material for a book. The premise was simple; I would follow as many of the railway journeys undertaken by Victorian and Edwardian anglers as I could, and I would write about them. All I had to do was catch a few fish, gather some anecdotes and make a few wry observations about life before and after the cuts of Richard Beeching. For once I was smart enough to know how fortunate I was and – if I hadn't worked it out already – there were phone calls from envious pals to tell me. Most of them began with, 'sorry to hear about your marriage … you lucky bastard'.

The journeys varied enormously, but each destination had been popular in the days before the Second World War and was famed for its fish. These included the Loch Leven trout of Lake Vyrnwy in North Wales, blue sharks off the Cornish coast, barbel and pike in the Thames and the exquisite brownies and rainbows of the Derbyshire Wye. My itinerary, which was based through necessity around school holidays, also took in a weekend on Windermere. I didn't expect to encounter any ferox en route, but they found me nonetheless.

I went to the Lake District in June. It was the beginning of the coarse fishers' year and the holiday season, and every instinct told me I should be on a southern tench lake. But my host was a busy man and it was to be that weekend or none at all. His name was Tim Berry.

We quickly established that we were probably not related, which saddened me more than it did Tim. He was a millionaire hotel owner with a lakeside water sports business and a traditional charr boat of his own, and was exactly the sort of chap I hoped might be found in the outer branches of the family tree – but it was not to be. He was good company and we spent an engrossing morning on his 100-year-old clinker, *Emily*, trailing long lines of spinners on ash poles in search of *salvelinus alpinus*. We caught very little, but it didn't matter. Tim had much to say about the glory days of commercial charr fishing on Windermere and was as entertaining a boatman as I could have wished for, but his stories belong elsewhere.

At dawn the following day I fished for roach to while away the time before my train was due. The fish were shoaled up around a private jetty – Tim's jetty, in fact – and were naive to the perils of float-fished bread. They were bright, silver specimens with deep red fins and some of them weighed close to a pound. I had mixed feelings about their presence, knowing that their resurgence had been at the expense of the indigenous charr and perch, but it was a pleasant way to wait for a train and I enjoyed the solitude.

The early morning mist began to dissipate and eventually the roach lost interest. As the sun gained strength and the clouds thinned, a clinker chugged across Low Wray Bay towards the northern shore. I heard it before I saw it and recognised the low gurgle of a boat at trolling speed – a sound I knew instantly, even after ten years. When it got closer I could see a pair of hefty rods at right angles to the boat and two long lines disappearing into the depths behind. Both rods were set in an unmoving, fishless bend, and that was familiar, too. I watched the boat for half an hour, and when it made for shore I followed it.

The solitary occupant beached 300 yards away, and by the time I reached him his rods were stowed and his outboard lying on the soft grass above the waterline. The angler – late forties, grey-haired, weather-beaten and unsmiling – was busily emptying his boat. There was quite a pile of equipment on the shore when I arrived – lures and camera bags and an echo sounder with GPS. But, if he was serious about his fishing, he was less keen to talk about it.

'Any good?'

'Bit quiet.'

'No trout then?'

'Trout? Nope.'

'Yes, ferox. I assumed you were after them.'

'Nope. Pike. No ferox trout in here.'

'Oh, right. I'd heard there were a few.'

I remembered Watson's book and the stories of 8-pounders, but I didn't mention them.

'Maybe there are,' he conceded. 'It's a big lake.'

'I used to fish for ferox myself once, that's all.' It felt odd saying it out loud, but it was true.

'Really?' He looked up at me now, with a suggestion of a smile.

'Yes, in Scotland and Ireland.'

'Not local then?'

'No, just visiting. Off home in the next hour.'

'I see.'

He relaxed then and we began to talk in full sentences, and less guardedly. He had, of course, been trolling for ferox trout, though none had come to the boat that morning, and he went after them quite frequently between Easter and October. I learnt that the water-skiers and holidaymakers could be an irritation and that fishing into dusk and beyond was better, 'when the tourists are away getting pissed up in Bowness'. He told me that the boat was his own and that the holiday industry meant that hire boats were priced extortionately. 'If you can buy a boat and find somewhere in the northern bays to moor it, you're halfway there.'

He paused then, as if he had said too much. I asked about methods but my companion's evasiveness had returned. 'It's all trolling. Deadbaits, lures and spinners, you know … nothing really works, anyway …'

It was only when we had shaken hands and wished each other luck that the man confessed to having ever caught a Windermere trout. He pulled a picture from his bag and handed it to me, saying, 'you should come back one day and try to catch one of these'. The photograph had been taken at night, and the ferox in his arms was as big as any I'd ever seen. The fish was heavily spotted, deep bodied and had a tail as big as a man's hand. I asked what it weighed but my new friend was as vague as ever. 'It was big enough,' he said, with the widest of grins.

As the TransPennine Express took me east and then south, I thought about ferox trout and the men who chased them, and how infuriatingly enigmatic both could be. I also began to wonder whether I ought to try to catch another. I had time, after all.

21

THE ROAD TO OUGHTERARD

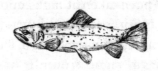

There was a dead dog in the road, splayed across the scorched tarmac. A mile further on another hapless mongrel, smaller but just as lifeless, lay in the gutter. The agrarian landscape was flat, the sun relentless, and my mind was beginning to conjure with the scenery outside our car. I hadn't seen a soul for some time and the single-storey buildings appeared deserted, shutters down. For a moment I thought I might be lost in the American Midwest, but I was not. I was on a back road between Tullamore and Athlone, and on my way to Lough Corrib.

Next to me, fast asleep, was Victoria. She had been an English teacher at the same school as me when my marriage had imploded, and over the subsequent months we had grown close – so much so that we had moved into a 300-year-old cottage together and decorated it with books and bamboo fishing rods. Freddy had joined us, securing a permanent spot in the summer house where he could stare hungrily out at the rabbits that lived on the lawn.

Life, finally, was idyllic. When I had explained that I needed to try to catch one more ferox trout, Vic had understood.

We had left Wiltshire at ten o'clock the previous night and driven through light rain and wind to the Pembrokeshire coast. The ferry to Rosslare had been crowded, and stumbling, singing drunks had ruined any chance of a catnap in the second-class lounge. Now we were driving slowly and with a questionable sense of direction through the middle of the Republic, and I had been awake for thirty hours. Helpfully, the fan beneath the bonnet of the Peugeot – a more recent model, but still in its second decade – had decided to shear off from its spindle 3 miles out of Kilkenny, and so the engine was continually overheating. The beginning of our Irish ferox adventure was less than glamorous.

We picked up the N6 at Athlone at lunchtime. Signs for Galway became more frequent and the topography began to undulate. The land was greener, the air fresher from the Atlantic breeze, and Vic began to remark on how beautiful it all was. I hadn't been this far west in a long time. Twelve years had passed since I had fished Lough Derg with Ricky and Anna. I had wanted to go to Galway and Connemara then, but we had travelled in Anna's car and with Anna's money and so she had picked our destination. This time the choice had been all mine.

I knew that if I was to try to catch a ferox, I had better go to the huge limestone loughs of the Irish Republic. Much had been written in the years since the Alness gang had disbanded about the great trout of Galway and Connemara. The ferox secret was out and what had once been a cult was now a growing subculture within the sport. The great majority continued to ignore the species, but ferox tyros were no longer considered mindless, trolling pariahs – just harmless oddballs in a sport where idiosyncrasies were the norm.

I couldn't be sure, but it just seemed that in Ireland there were more fish to be caught. I planned to visit the Highlands later in the year but this was the first week of June, the half-term holidays, and Vic was with me; Irish pubs and Gaelic charm could fill each evening and I knew that the west coast offered great beauty which my girl would enjoy. If I was smart it could seem less like an endurance test and more like a holiday – sleepless nights and dead dogs notwithstanding.

A number of Irish loughs held ferox trout, but Mask and Corrib offered our best chance. Both had long histories of charr and giant trout, of deep water and limestone plateaus, of islands and secrets. There were boatmen on each who could take me to the fish and provide the kind of knowledge that was earned in decades rather than days. It would be different to the war of attrition we had waged in Sutherland, more of a hit-and-run affair – and I only wanted to land one.

That prospect became real when I heard about Patrick Molloy. He operated out of Oughterard on Corrib's west coast and was the last of many generations of Molloys who had fished and worked the lough. Molloy had thirteen years' experience of tagging *salmo ferox* on Corrib and Mask for the Irish Fisheries Board, and there were photographs in his brochure that left me speechless. I called him early in the year and asked about my prospects for a week at the beginning of June. 'A whole week to catch one? No bother. As long as it's calm, mind – no bother at all.'

I wasn't sure that I believed him; three years in the Highlands had taught me that ferox rarely lent themselves to instant gratification, but I booked his services for five days all the same.

We spoke several times in the month before Vic and I were due to arrive. There were high winds and volcanic ash in the air, and Patrick was preoccupied with Corrib's mayfly hatches and the smaller trout for which the lough was famous. He hadn't been out for the ferox yet, but every time I called he repeated his promise – 'no bother at all, as long as it's calm'.

Ten days before our departure, Patrick called for the last time. A group of Czech anglers had been stranded in Galway at the start of the month, waiting for the Icelandic cloud to dissipate, and they had taken to trolling. One of them, a gentleman named Karel Sourek, had landed a 25lb fish on a lure; it was the largest Irish ferox in a century and only ounces from being a national record. 'They're starting to feed, Jon,' Patrick said. 'We'll get you your trophy.' I told him I would be overjoyed with one half that size, but suspected even that was asking for a little too much.

For Ricky and I, our ferox hunt had never been about breaking records. The rarity and beauty of the fish was such that each was regarded as a prize. The smaller fish that we had caught at Shin and Veyatie, the 2- and 3-pounders, were still remarkable brown trout. Five-pounders had us shaking with excitement. They were all magnificent.

I had been keen to avoid the obsessive gigantism that had sullied carp fishing. Ricky was accustomed to the wee brownies of the burns and lochs and so he had never lost a sense of perspective. But we were fishermen: an appreciation of the larger, scarcer specimens was inevitable. We didn't often talk of it, but both of us thought of double-figure ferox – 10-pounders and above – as the fish of our dreams. It was these I thought of as Vic and I got closer to Corrib.

Galway came and went. Vic wanted to see the city and its canals, its harbour and its medieval architecture, but the N6 fed into the N59 and bypassed the best of it, so I promised we would return during the week. We drove north and passed through settlements with the most Irish of names; places called Killola, Cloonnabinnia and Gortnamona West, and the fabulously moniker-ered Porridgetown. And then the road swung down to the deep water of Corrib's northern bay and we were in Oughterard.

Lough Corrib is the second largest lake on the Irish mainland; only Lough Neagh to the west of Belfast is bigger. The visitor driving out of Galway City sees the southern bay first, where Corrib ends and joins a river of the same name. Here the lough is modest, relatively open and home to vast shoals of brown trout which rise each year to the duck fly and mayfly. It is shallow, between 6 and 10ft, and rich in weed.

At Curra Point the lough begins to narrow and islands proliferate. Here, Corrib is an intimate, welcoming place and from the water each bay and island can seem like a world of its own. Only at Carraghmore Point does the lough's enormity become apparent. From Oughterard in the west to Cong and the River Maam in the north, upper Corrib can resemble an inland sea. The comparison has been made many times and, this being Ireland, there is a story about it.

The tale is told by the lough's finest chronicler, Sir William Robert Wilde – archaeologist, surgeon, author and father of Oscar. Wilde Senior holidayed at the lough and, in the manner of well-to-do Victorians, had a summerhouse built there. His book, *Lough Corrib; its Shores and Islands: with notices of Lough Mask* (1867), gave the definitive explanation of the naming of the lake.

According to Wilde, the lough was first known as Orbsen, after Orbsen Mac Alloid, a mortal incarnation of Manannan Mac Lir, the Lord of the Sea. Legend has it that Orbsen engaged in combat with a warrior known as Uillen Red Edge at Moycullen, now on the lough's western shore. The former was defeated and the lough appeared where his blood was spilled. Thus in death, Manannan created a sea of his own.

Wilde took Corrib to be a corruption of Orib, which in turn was probably a localised variation on Orbsen. He was probably correct, but if he was not, it matters little; Wilde's explanation has been absorbed into local lore – which makes it as good as true.

Corrib features in much of the mythology of the west, and this is testimony to the importance of its waters to early settlers in Galway and Connemara. Its size and dominance of the landscape are astonishing enough to a twenty-first-century visitor; for primitive peoples it would have been the source of food and water, the provider of building materials and the very centre of their world. It is hardly surprising, then, that the lough took on a more spiritual significance. There were said to be gods residing in palaces below its surface and *merrow* – a celtic form of mermaid – swimming in its depths. No mention was ever made, though, of the shoals of ferox which would have been present throughout.

Not all of Corrib's fanciful stories date back to Ireland's prehistory. As recently as 2005, the bats living in Ashford Castle were said to possess a preternatural talent for predicting the weather. Allegedly, the position in which the bats hung from pipes in the

boiler room indicated whether the days would be wet or dry, settled or otherwise. Vic and I were to hear similar fanciful claims
throughout our week there and each of them seemed plausible
enough to us. Whether this was because of the magic of our surroundings, the unseen influence of celtic gods or the quality of the
local stout was unclear.

Corrib, like its neighbour Mask and many of the larger loughs
in Ireland, is ostensibly a limestone lake. Huge plateaus and shelves
are found below the surface and the shores of many of its islands
are made up of dry, eroded and sulphurous boulders that suggest
a desolate moonscape. There is granite and sandstone, too, and the
deep water where the ferox live is clear and cold.

The lough sits in a mixed landscape. The west is mountainous,
the east a patchwork of flat plains. The north-west beyond Maam
Cross is high and dotted with lochans and free-running rivers,
and resembles some of the finest parts of the Scottish Highlands.
Beyond Cong, at Corrib's most northerly point, are Lough Mask
and a new world of secrets. The shores of the lough are heavily
forested and sparsely populated, and the sheer slopes of the uplands
reflect and magnify every change in the sun.

It is also wild and the waves that Patrick had warned us of can
be formidable. On angry days the white caps can reach 10ft high.
In heavy flood, levels can rise suddenly and swallow up islands.
High winds can whip the surface into tornadoes of foam and on
such days the far shore can disappear from view. Boats can vanish,
men too.

Later in the week Vic and I would be taken to an island grave and
told of a young fisherman who perished only yards from its shore,
but his story was one among many. For all its beauty, Corrib has
always been too big, too deep and too moody to be tamed by man.
For centuries, locals have known not to take the lough for granted,
and when it has claimed one of their own they have mourned quietly and regretted that Manannan had taken another of their number.

If Corrib is a lough of mythology and beauty, it is also one with
a peerless angling tradition. It has been fished for its trout ever since

man took a boat on to its waters, and its fame has extended beyond the Irish mainland for at least a century. Salmon run its length, pike grow to frightening proportions in the depths and there is a considerable (and largely unwelcome) population of silver fish. But it is the trout for which Corrib has long been revered. Modern anglers fish with buzzers and mayflies, nymphs and wets, but the proper way to fish for the browns is 'on the dap'. Natural baits are fished in the surface film on long, reel-less rods, and with gossamer lines. It is a method that has been used on Irish waters for longer than anyone can remember and, in late May and early June, it can be deadly.

Such is the popularity of dapping that a local cottage industry has long existed to serve the angler. Each May, schoolchildren are given respite from their studies to collect the large, long-tailed flies from waterside trees and bushes, and sell them in boxes to visiting anglers. It is a quaint and dignified tradition – unless, of course, you happen to be a mayfly – and could only be imagined in the west of Ireland.

If Corrib had not been named in memory of a mythical Lord of the Sea, it would have been called something like the Lough of Many Islands, or at least a prettier Gaelic variation on the same. From the shallow waters of the upper lough to the northernmost point at Ashford Castle, they are everywhere. Most are small, some little more than outcrops of rock that disappear whenever the lough rises, but others are significant and perhaps ten are inhabited. A few have wind turbines and at least one has a helipad.

Inchagoil, between Oughterard and Cong, is the most celebrated and looks out to Joyce country and the mountains of Connemara. Two churches can be found there, as well as the ruins of houses and a cemetery. Locals claim that the island was an early monastic settlement, but the history of its Order is vague. Now, Inchagoil receives visitors from the steamers that work the lough and is a landmark for all who chase the ferox.

Almost half of the islands are named. Inchiquin, Inchagoil and Inishdoorus are well known, but there are others whose titles vary depending on who you ask or which map you consult. There are two (possibly three) Rabbit Islands, a Goat Island, a Prison Island and one which – with a grasp of spelling befitting an American politician – is called simply Potatoe. A brief troll of one north-eastern bay will take you past Green Island, Red Island, Whiskey and Dog Islands, and another known only as Morris. Between Cong and Curry Point your boat will pass three different Black Rocks. But a different map could tell you otherwise, and this can lead to confusion in the bar whenever fishermen gather.

'You caught it off Rory's Island? Sure, that's not Rory's, it's called Malachy's Dog, always has been … Rory's is that bigger fellah with the trees on that your man over there calls Inishgobshite.'

But if the people of Corrib cannot agree on what each of the islands is called, there is at least consensus on their number. We heard the same claim wherever we went, afloat and on dry land, and it echoed the words of Sir William Wilde in 1867:

> The islands of Lough Corrib are so numerous, that the people of the district say they number 365, or one for every day of the year, and that an additional one rises on leap year.

At the start of the week I thought about sitting in an Oughterard pub with my map and counting each and every island, but somehow – like generations of locals and visitors before me – I never did find the time. We were on a lough of astonishing history and beauty, and there were giant brown trout there, too.

22

A WEEK ON THE CORRIB

When I suggested that we should go to Ireland, I had envisaged camping on the lough shore each night. It would be romantic, wild and free in every respect. Vic thought differently and so, on Patrick Molloy's advice, we arranged to stay at Lal Faherty's. Lal's offered en suite rooms, boat launches, a turf fire and views over the lough at Oughterard. It was close to our ghillie's own mooring and also to the town, and this suited Vic, who had no intention of spending five long days afloat.

It was a perfect spot. The mayfly had vanished and so too had the annual influx of fly fishermen, and we had the pick of the rooms. Ours looked out through French windows towards the jetty where Lal moored his team of clinkers and we could see a hundred acres of water without leaving our bed. Just outside our door was the fishermen's lounge. A stuffed ferox of 10lb glowered from a bow-fronted case on the wall and Vic could at last see why we had travelled for two sleepless days across the British Isles.

Lal was missing and we would not see him all week. The mayfly had gone and so had he, and business was temporarily in the hands of his son-in-law, Gary Costello. The stand-in host greeted us warmly and assured us that Patrick was just the man to lead us to a ferox trout. There was a brief, knowing laugh when he said this, just a hint of mischief that said, 'and I know what you're in for'. Gary gave us a message from our boatman – *be at the jetty at nine on Monday morning and don't be late* – and then he left us, still chuckling quietly as he walked away.

Vic and I went into the town in the evening. It was small, pretty and surprisingly lively. Two shops offered food and tourist goods but most of its old stone buildings appeared to be bars or takeaways; if the business of Oughterard was fishing, the townspeople knew their clientele well. We wandered aimlessly and found ourselves in Breathnach's, a small bar dating back to 1839 with stuffed fish and photographs on its walls. I ordered Guinness and food, and since neither arrives quickly in Ireland we read the handwritten descriptions on each picture. Most recorded impressive catches of smaller trout, but a few showed grinning, bewildered men holding up larger prizes. Some were recent, others sepia-tinted and stained with smoke. I spotted the name Molloy more than once.

The sun had set by the time we returned to Lal's, but there was a prescient glow on the water and we could see the faintest of ripples. We were restless and sleep came fitfully. In the early hours I sat on the veranda, looking out on the lough, and wondered whether, after eleven years, I might just catch another ferox trout.

Morning came and Gary walked down with me to the jetty. One of his dogs, an inquisitive beagle, joined us to see what the fuss was about. Patrick was not due for another half an hour but I had risen at first light and was keen to be afloat. The water was calm in front of us, but Gary was sceptical about our chances of trolling. Lal's bay was sheltered by Portcarron Point and the lough would be rougher out towards Inchiquin. He offered to run back to the house and get me a fly rod, but I was having none of it. I had driven a long way to fish for ferox trout and that was exactly what I intended to do. 'Sure,' said the host. 'Patrick won't mind either way.'

Shortly before nine o'clock we heard a boat making its way around the point at speed, and as it cut into the bay and slowed up a green clinker came into view. It was *Mayfly*, and the skipper at the helm was the big, balding man in Arran that I had seen in pictures. He pulled in, tied up and then shook my hand firmly. 'So you're the ferox man, are ye? You'd be better off on the fly today boy.'

Gary intervened. 'He's having none of it, Patrick. His mind is on a big one and nothing else.' They both laughed and exchanged a glance, while I took up my spot on the centre thwart and wondered whether my desperation was obvious. The ghillie was soon ready and pushed us gently out on to the clear, cold waters of Corrib.

Patrick was talkative from the off, telling me about the islands and the shoals of roach which the ferox fed upon, but I struggled at first with his accent and nodded like a fool above the noise of the outboard. The sky was clear but for a few stray clouds and the temperature on the water was mild – more spring than summer but not unpleasant. We motored past the first islands, up the lough towards the north, passing Creeve, Inishdawee and Roeillaun before changing direction and pointing north-east towards the underwater plateau of the Bilberry shallows. Only then did Patrick slow the engine to a gentle tickover and announce that we could begin.

Dead roach baits were mounted on treble hooks and fed on long lines into the water 100 yards behind the boat. Rods were mounted in holders, nets stowed close to hand. Finally, Patrick was ready to issue a solemn declaration. 'OK,' he said, 'now we are fishing.'

I smiled at this. Ricky had often said the same thing.

We trolled steadily for a morning, exploring the water off the many smaller islands between Inchiquin and Inchagoil. It was calm enough, rougher than it had been in the bay at Lal's, but not so bad that we couldn't maintain a regular course. Patrick assured me that conditions were fine and that we ought to 'get among them' at some point during my stay. 'Sure, I've gone six days without a fish before now, but that was awful rare,' he said. 'Just you sit there and wait.'

Waiting was something I knew how to do. The landscape was unfamiliar and the contrast with the Highland lochs mesmerising. Kildermorie and Veyatie had been deep, narrow and overlooked by mountains; Shin stark and grey and magnificent in its isolation. Separation from them had served only to exaggerate their features in my memory. Corrib was so different. Its great width flattened the horizon around it; its populated islands gave it an intimacy that belied its size. It was only when I stared into the dark glacial water that it felt like the places I had known in Sutherland and Easter Ross.

But the fishing was familiar. The low, gurgling buzz of the outboard was the same as it had always been, the gentle curve of stationary rods was as mocking as ever. Time passed slowly, deliciously so, heavy with expectation and hope. Nothing happened, until it did.

'Fish on,' I cried. The rod to my right had moved in its holder and was pulsing in a quarter circle.

All had been quiet and now everything happened at once. The ghillie revved the engine and set the hooks; I wound down and found life on the end of a long line and, in the distance beyond our wake, something pulled back. It was one o'clock and we had been fishing for less than four hours.

And so the first battle of Corrib began. We saw nothing of the fish for an age as it zipped and dived and clung to the bedrock. Patrick shouted instructions and I did my best to follow them, but it was many nervous minutes before the fish surfaced, gasping and desperate. Patrick lifted the prop and went for the net, and then, in a flourish of golds and spots and spray, it was over. The ghillie shook my hand and we made for the nearside shore of Mucklagh.

Patrick wanted to take the fish and so he administered its last rites with a priest and then we weighed and photographed it. The trout was long, slim but not hollow, dark and heavily spotted. It weighed 11lb.

I sat on the limestone shore of the island and thought about Ricky, the Alness boys and Scotland, while Patrick made two mugs of black tea. Sutherland was far away and a long time ago, but in that sublime moment it felt closer than it had in years. I remembered Polly and Sween and the old man at Shin, and I remembered the Highlands, too. But above all, I thought about those long days of trolling, those endless blank days of trolling …

It was my companion who brought me out of my reverie. 'OK now, get yer arse in the boat and we'll see if we can't catch another.'

We retraced our wake from the morning, along the drop-offs and among the islands in the widest part of the lough, and in the middle of the afternoon there was a pull on the other rod. The fish fought as ferociously as the first, running and diving and trying to break me off below the boat. When it finally surfaced and rolled close to the net, fifteen minutes after being hooked, we saw its depth for the first time. Even the ghillie was impressed. 'For feck's sake, will you look at the size o' him!' he cried. The second ferox trout of the day weighed 12½lb.

There were to be no more chances, but it didn't matter. Patrick and I talked about the lough and its fish, about the richness of the water and the prodigious giant trout. I learnt about the cormorants and otters, about the ancient folk who had lived on the islands and about the ghillie himself. The big west coast sky clouded over during the afternoon but I didn't notice until the rain came, heavily and horizontally, at five o'clock. We made for shore and agreed to continue our search in the morning.

Mayfly and its skipper rounded the bay as the sun rose on the following day. Patrick was early but I was waiting for him. Two fish had already come to the boat, more than I had hoped for in a week, but we were fishermen and were not about to ignore the possibility of more. Patrick cut his engine, just as he had twenty-four hours earlier, and drifted quietly in. This time he called out to me.

'I opened the door this morning and saw the sky and thought I'd come straight to you. It looks good out there!'

It did. Lal's bay was calm and the sky promised warmth later in the day, but it was a false dawn in every sense. The fickle west coast weather soon changed its mind and by the time we reached the islands, the wind had switched from west to north-west and there was a formidable chop on the water. The bow of our boat plunged and lifted with each wave. We fished the water that had been so kind to us previously, but the first hours were uneventful. There were no pulls or enquiries.

We did what all ferox fishermen do. We trolled and we waited, and we trolled some more. We watched the water for signs of life and sucked air through our teeth in thought. The reluctance of the fish to bite also gave us time to talk and I learnt a little more about my companion.

Patrick and his brothers all worked the lough, as generations of Molloys had done before them, but the ghillie also fought fires in the hills and farmed the land around him. He still tagged the trout on Corrib and Mask when the Fisheries Board needed him to, and he was able to show me the rivers where the ferox ran to spawn in the autumn.

Late in the morning we passed an island where Patrick had worked as a child, rowing out after school each day to pick potatoes. There were times, he said, when the boat hadn't been there and he'd had to swim it. I thought I sensed a little blarney, but knew better than to say so. On a long, quiet day, a ghillie's yarn is always better than the truth.

At lunchtime, as we skirted an island looking for somewhere to beach, I had a small pluck. It wasn't one of the unmissable wrenches of the previous day, more a tentative increase in the rod's curve, but I hit it anyway and made contact. The fish came to the boat in five minutes.

It was smaller, as we had suspected, but beautiful – hundreds of tiny black spots, chestnut flanks with just a hint of gold. We didn't weigh it but estimated it at 6lb, much the same as the fish which had started all the trouble thirteen years ago. Patrick took a quick photograph and the fish was slipped back only seconds after it had been netted. It went off quickly and deeply, and in the shallow water off the island we were able to watch it dive to the bottom.

After lunch we continued searching the deep water near the islands, but all was quiet and by sunset we knew that there would be no more trout. Patrick called his brothers, who had been trolling all day, and they had no fish to report. We returned to Lal's and agreed that our third day would be spent elsewhere, in the deep open water of the north around Cong. I reminded Patrick that Vic would be coming out with us for the day.

'OK, so she is,' said the ghillie, 'then we will have a feast at lunchtime. You leave it to me, boy.'

Patrick picked us both up at 8.30 a.m. the next day, opened up the throttle of the big Honda engine and took us to the far end of the lough. It was quite a ride, all spray and bumps and deft weaving between islands, and I wondered at first whether he was showing off to Vic. I then realised what was on our ghillie's mind. On the first day, Patrick had told me about a giant fish he had hooked and lost up there, and we were now visiting the scene of some unfinished business. We were on a monster hunt.

The ghillie dropped the engine to tick over when the shore at Cong came into view and told us that we could begin. We trolled hard for three hours, with big baits and more lead to take the lines down further. Patrick relaxed and adjusted to Vic's presence; there was less swearing, some clean jokes, no pissing into the baler, but he still had an air of Captain Quint about him and I wondered just how big the lost fish had been.

I had two hesitant enquiries close to Queen's Rock during the morning, but the trout were merely taunting us. The lough was calmer than it had been all week, and the sky was high and cloudless. This suited Vic, who was happy to sleep and read, but was less appealing to the fish. When we beached for our midday feast, in a silent bay on Canaver, the vista was distinctly Caribbean.

Lunch was quite magnificent: generous lamb cuts from Patrick's own flock, with wild onions and garlic, peppers, mushrooms and potatoes – all of it pulled from the earth around Corrib. We built a fire and crowned it with Patrick's huge blackened frying pan; Vic collected wood and made strong black tea for us all.

There was a headstone in the scrub behind us and after lunch Vic read out the inscription. It said: 'To the memory of Barry Quinn, Castlecrine, Sixmilebridge, County Clare, who drowned tragically off Canaver Island on 22nd March 2003, aged 28 years.

He was one of life's gentlemen who loved nature and all sport – especially fishing.'

As we finished the dregs of our tea, Patrick told us a little of the story – of the lad's attempt to swim out to his boat when it drifted from the shore, of the coldness of the water that day and the likelihood that the young man's heart had given way. He told us that it was he and a friend who had pulled the body of Barry Quinn from the lough, and we knew then why our ghillie had brought us to Canaver. We raised our mugs in silent tribute, and then we returned to the water.

It was not a day for catching fish and by early evening we were back at Lal's. I took Vic to Galway and we found a pub overlooking a canalised river which ran into the estuary. Its water looked dirty and lifeless, but the seal that swam only yards from our table thought otherwise. The city was all life, colour and noise. It was Gomorrah after Eden, and we loved it.

The water was calm at sunrise. There was less heat and more cloud cover and this made all the difference. By 9.30 a.m. Patrick and I had caught and returned two ferox, of 6 and 7lb. Both took in open water between Mucklagh and the Bilberry Shallows. They were markedly different fish. The larger was black and silver with a broad tail and butter-coloured belly. The smaller was all coppers and golds. Both fought ferociously, and were beautiful.

The wind rose during the morning and by midday we were back at Lal's with an angry lough behind us. Vic was pleased that we had an unexpectedly free afternoon and so we took the north-west road out to Clifden, an exquisitely appointed seaside town with a distinctly bohemian feel to it. We wandered the boutiques and antique shops, but their prices had little in common with the summer of love and were more reminiscent of Gordon Gekko's eighties. We left entranced, but curious about the sort of person who would spend €150 on a vintage lava lamp.

The day ended at another bar, further down the same road as Breathnach's. A young folk guitarist was performing, nervously but with conviction, to an audience of six. We stayed and cheered him on until he had no songs left to play, and then we cheered some more. The black stuff was entirely culpable.

Patrick collected me for the last time at dawn on the Friday. The water was choppy when we started and grew steadily more unpleasant, and we agreed that we would finish at lunch so that Vic and I could drive across Ireland and be on the south-east coast by supper.

The worsening weather kept us close to shore, around the shallower waters of Currarevagh and Kitteen's Bay. We took off some of the lead, knowing that we were likely to snag up all the same, and when one of the rods pulled round at eleven o'clock I was sure we were into weed. I wound down and Patrick slowed up ready to reverse, but the rod bucked and thumped and something unseen began to strip my reel of line.

'Jesus boy, that's the one you were after,' said Patrick. There was a nervous whisper to his voice that I had not heard all week.

The fish felt monstrous, and it was, but when it surfaced 50 yards from the boat we saw that it was pike-shaped. The thick nylon trace held among its teeth and, after a minor tug of war, Patrick scooped it up and into the boat with little ceremony. We were impressed with its size, but to the ghillie it was a trout-eating impostor. He declared it only good for feeding cats and wives. And then he bashed it on the head.

We took it back to Lal's and weighed it at exactly 20lb, and then Patrick disappeared round Portcarron Point and was gone, with a pocketful of Euro and a fish large enough to feed as many wives and cats as he wished. I left him with an unhooking mat and a very English perspective on the value of pike, and hoped he would find use for both.

Vic was there and we were sad to see him go. The success of our adventure had rested squarely upon the choice of ghillie, and we had been very fortunate in securing the services of Patrick Molloy. He had been more than a fisherman to us. He had been an alchemist.

On our last afternoon we drove across an ancient land and crossed the Irish Sea, leaving the beauty of Corrib and its people behind us. I had my scribbled notes, a handful of photographs and vivid memories of the trout and the ghillie. Vic and I had our shared memories, too – Clifden, Galway, the solitude of Canaver – and we were grateful for them.

We had travelled to Ireland to catch a solitary ferox, but in the end it was unremarkable that we caught five, or that two of them had been large. On the numinous water of Corrib, it could be regarded only as a minor miracle. Men who lived and worked on the lough and absorbed its waters into their souls, men like Patrick Molloy, understood. The fishermen came and filled their nets, filled their hearts, too, and then left. They stuck their photographs to the walls of the bars and enjoyed the glory of a catch, and told their friends about the wonderful trout of the Corrib. But the fish themselves just lived on, as they had for thousands of years – through ice and heat, flood and drought, through the decline of the charr and the ascendancy of the roach, through pollution and plenty.

On a ferry in the middle of the Irish Sea, and in the first hours of the new day, I worked it out. It was not a miracle that we caught some. It was a miracle that they were there at all.

23

A GATHERING
OF THE CLAN

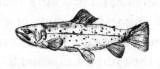

It was my mother's idea. When my brother and I left home, she took on the roles of clan chief, disseminator of information and organiser of knees-ups. She became a benevolent despot with a glass of pinot in one hand and a manifesto of family unity in the other, and we all knew better than to argue when she formulated a plan. This one was among her best; we would meet in the summer at a cottage in Ross-shire, close to Ricky and to the river, to Fyrish and the lochs, and we would enjoy ourselves in the way of the Frasers – by water, on mountains, in drink. An instruction from the clan chief was not for negotiation; it would be so.

So Vic and I drove north in August. We stopped in Lincolnshire to meet up with my brother and his son, Edward, and formed a two-car convoy into the Highlands. The old Peugeot was no match for my brother's shiny, high-end saloon and they lost us somewhere on the A9, but by late afternoon we had reconvened at the designated cottage, 50 yards from a loch and 3 miles from Ricky.

My mother poured the gin and tonics. We boys ran down to the water.

The loch was small, dammed, more farm pool than glacial legacy, and thick with weed from top to bottom. Rainbow trout, finger-length at best, cruised lazily on its surface. My brother and I agreed that in another setting it would have made a fine carp lake, but our fishing for the week would have to take place elsewhere. The grilse were running the Averon and there were brownies in the burns.

I was desperate to drive into Sutherland, too, and stare once more into the deep water of Shin. There was no ferox tackle in the car – no sounder, no lures or trebles, no long powerful rods – and being there would have to be enough. The five Corrib fish had gone some way towards satisfying a long-standing curiosity and I knew I could always go back to Galway, but long days trolling in the Highlands were not part of my mother's plan.

Edward was 10 and already an experienced fisher-boy. He had caught large carp and barbel, tench in great numbers and we had once shared the landing of a pike of 17lb. But he knew his Uncle Ricky was a proper fisherman – a fly fisherman who could stride into a river and walk out again with a salmon – and that was what he wanted to do. The casting lessons began on the lawn of the cottage on the first afternoon.

By the following morning he had declared himself an expert, and though this was not yet true he was able to put out a long and straight line across the grass. His father and I agreed he was ready to land a fly on water, though not the bouldered pools of the Averon. Not yet.

I suggested we visit the same rainbow trout fishery that Ricky and I had been to years before, when we had been blown off Shin. Enough time had passed to dim the memory of its pay-by-the-hour ruthlessness and I chose instead to remember its treeless banks and gullible fish. On a hot afternoon it would offer Edward his best chance of a fly-caught trout.

The lake had matured and was almost beautiful. It was only at the water's edge, beneath a fringe of reeds, that the scrapes of the diggers were still evident. Young trees now lined the water and a sign by the clubhouse announced that the fishing, due to the transgressions of a minority, was strictly 'fly only'. Rainbow trout could be seen rising freely and we were advised to fish fine and 'match the hatch'.

A decade earlier, everyone had been using maggots with bubble floats.

We fished sedges and olives throughout a lazy afternoon and we caught fish, but they were harder to tempt than we might have expected. Catch and Release policies had made them skittish and it was only the right pattern and a good, subtle cast that could elicit a take. Finally, Edward landed his first fly-caught trout, and we drove to Ricky's so that the young expert could tell the master his story.

The following day was given over to the centrepiece of mother's grand plan. We groaned and grumbled and developed sudden infirmities, but the chief was deaf to our protests. The clan was to gather on the eastern slope of Fyrish and find its way to Hector's monument, 1,400ft above the town where my mother was born, where Baldy marched off to war and where Ricky taught Chris and I to fish. And so the clan did as it was told.

We took photographs at its summit, huddled beneath the arches of Munro's Indian folly, and looked north to the peaks of Easter Ross. Somewhere out there was Kildermorie and Loch Glass, among the heather-strewn lands tamed by old Hector, but the valleys were lost in mist.

The chief fed the clan with the last of the chocolate in her handbag and we descended, each of us feeling that, somehow, we had done something that mattered, even if we didn't know what.

Halfway down we crossed a bridge over a tumbling burn, one of the countless streams that fed the Averon, and eventually poured into the Cromarty Firth. The water was the same as that of the river, black from the rocks, malt brown from the earth around it, clear and yet full of colour and life. Tiny trout zipped about its pools. We stared into it for an age and I told Vic how glad I was to have shared the moment with her.

For three days we fished and drank and ate. Ricky and Fran joined us at the cottage and my brother tried for salmon in the Stick

Pool, without success. Edward talked of brown trout and burns, and so his father took him to the stream that ran into Dalnacloich and his questions were answered. We drove out to Bodle's Burn one afternoon, to the spot where two brothers' story had begun over thirty years earlier, but the woods had been consumed by a housing estate and the magical waters from where we had taken our first fish had shrunk to a littered trickle in the shadow of a by-pass. It was a low moment in a week that was otherwise joyful.

Edward wanted to cast a line with Ricky, and his father and I were keen that he did. Our cousin was not well and adventures on the river would not have been sanctioned by Fran, but there were other kinds of fishing to be had on the east coast. Vic and I knew just the place and so, at dawn on our fifth morning, we drove out to Cromarty Pier.

The village of Cromarty sits on the southern shore of the firth, opposite Alness and Invergordon and in the shadows of the oil rigs at Nigg. Its distance from the A9 is such that tourists rarely visit, and the white stone fishermen's cottages hark back to an earlier age. For Vic and me, it is our favourite place in Scotland.

The pier is a working one, all nets, boats and crates of crabs, but beneath its uprights are shoals of mackerel and coalfish. In the summer holidays it is festooned with pier rats – semi-feral kids with rods, hand-lines and deep tans – but the schools had started up again and on that day we were alone. We all caught fish, but the hierarchy of the pier is different to any other and the young angler always catches the most. Edward soon lost count of his bounty.

The tide turned and began to disappear by mid-morning, and Vic and I began to pack our rods away. Chris joined us, happy with his haul and ready for home. At the other end of the pier, Ricky and Edward sat on an upturned crate, hunched in conversation, pausing only to unhook their fish. The mountains looked over us and the Cromarty Firth stretched for miles in all directions, but for the man and the boy there was only the moment and the shoal in front of them. We watched the master with the young expert and we smiled. Edward would remember this day for a very long time.

On our last full day we drove out of Easter Ross and into Sutherland. We climbed the Electric Hill and passed the turning which had once led to Sween. The streets of Bonar and Ardross were quiet, dusty in the final days of summer, and the river below us at Dornoch ran low and clear. Edward wanted to see the Falls of Shin and so at Lairg we took the left turn into the mountains.

The café and shop were busy with tourists and wherever we looked there were reminders of Harrods and Mohammed al Fayed, who had, until recently, claimed to own this corner of the Highlands. I was reminded of Norman MacCaig's *A Man in Assynt*:

> Who owns this landscape? –
> The millionaire who bought it or
> The poacher staggering downhill in the early morning
> With a deer on his back?

> Who possesses this landscape? –
> The man who bought it or
> I who am possessed by it?

> False questions, for
> This landscape is masterless.

We took our place among the others on the platforms and watched the salmon as they scaled the falls in desperation, driven by every instinct to their spawning grounds and an inevitable death. Then, when we had seen enough, we drove to Shin.

The loch was flat, bathed in sunlight and empty of fishermen. The angling club hut was closed up for the day and we couldn't have fished even if we had wanted to, but that was not why we were there. I wanted to show Vic where the ferox story had begun, to sit on the shore and remember Donian and Polly and the rest of the boys. The green and white clinkers were pulled up on the rocks, just as they always had been; the far horizon was dotted with the same crofters' cottages and the grey outbuildings of the salmon farm. Nothing moved on the water, but that only added to the beauty. I knew, and so did my companions, that beneath the surface there were monsters.

We skimmed stones and took photographs. And before we turned our backs, we promised to return.

The gathering of the clan ended that night, and we woke with sore heads to rain and high winds. Vic and I left in haste. We had a long drive ahead of us, and there was one more place to go before home.

24

THE GURU

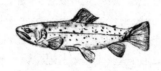

Two weeks before the journey to Scotland I had spoken with Ron Greer. Until that point, the ferox trout hunt had taken place in splendid isolation. We had known about the Pitlochry men and the small ferox cult of the Perthshire lochs, but Ricky, the Alness boys and I had orbited our own little universe in Sutherland and Easter Ross. We had met no other ferox fishermen on Shin, Kildermorie or Veyatie, only the old man who had guided us towards the black waters, and we had liked it that way. We followed hunches and whims and our only guidance had come from Victorian literature and Greer's book. But in the summer of 2010, I decided that it was time to make contact with the guru.

In the frighteningly open age of the World Wide Web, it was easy to do. A Mr R. Greer of Blair Atholl was a regular contributor to the online letters pages of *The Scotsman*. Each missive lambasted the folly of Holyrood's environmental policies, and did so with a familiar scientific and idiosyncratic vigour. I didn't think there could be two of them, and wrote to this Mr Greer. Twenty-four hours later, the guru replied.

We exchanged emails and telephone calls and Ron kindly sent me two of his more recent scientific papers. The first was called 'A Fish Inventory of River Spey Lochs using Multiple Mesh Size Gillnets – a first of its kind survey' (Ron B. Greer & Johann Hammer, 2004). The paper recorded work on the presence and effects of non-indigenous species in the lochs around Aviemore. The potentially catastrophic consequences of pike, roach, rudd and hatchery trout introductions on native charr and trout populations were detailed with scientific rigour and much passion.

The second paper was from a 2010 edition of *Hydrobiologia – The International Journal of Aquatic Sciences*. The piece, co-authored by Greer and three colleagues, had the kind of title only a fish scientist could conjure up: 'Mitochondrial DNA variation in Arctic charr morphs from Loch Rannoch, Scotland: evidence for allopatric and peripatric divergence' (Crown Copyright Marine Scotland, 2010).

The front page alone left me a little dizzy and once again I felt like an impostor stumbling upon a secret society. Nevertheless, I persevered with it and was enthralled. Greer and his colleagues described remarkable progress in identifying the ecologically and morphologically distinct forms of charr in Rannoch. It was heady stuff, of Darwinian importance to those who cared for the integrity of the Highland environment and its Ice Age fauna.

My O Level Science was stretched to its limit and beyond, but I was left in no doubt: the spirit of the young man who led the Loch Garry Tree Group had in no way diminished over time.

We met in a restaurant off the old A9. Greer was tall, familiar from the photographs in his book, with a moustache that hinted at a Highland Fu Manchu. I was apprehensive, but the guru put me at ease with good humour and a scurrilous tale about a stuffed stickleback.

The House of Bruar's dining room was given over to angling memorabilia and there were casts of 40lb salmon on every wall. Over coffee, we discussed the possibility of a Highland ferox trout reaching such a weight, and Ron told me that he was as mesmerised by the prospect of catching a record ferox as ever. He even told me where he hoped to do it. We talked of several lochs, some that I knew and others I did not, and of the fish I had landed from Lough Corrib.

The guru had to be out on the water with his gill nets later in the day, so I set up my tape recorder. I was already in deep water, scientifically speaking. Now I had to pretend to be a journalist.

An interview with Ron Greer, August 2010

JB: Fifteen years have passed since your book was published; what has happened to you professionally and in your fishing life since then?

RG: *Well, I went way out on a limb following another big land use project and it took me away from [ferox] for a while. I went on to other things connected to the strategic management of Highland land – from the northern perspective that the fish had given me. It's all related because the ferox and charr are just one aspect of the boreal inheritance of the Highlands that we don't fully appreciate. So I went away to do some work on that – some of it worked out, some of it didn't. Now I've come back round full circle to doing surveys on lakes that haven't been surveyed before. I'm back to angling for ferox again. I'm just starting on phase two.*

JB: And you're enjoying it?

RG: *Tremendously! I have never given up fishing, just the fanatical commitment that I had back in the '80s and '90s when it was three times a week, when it became an obsessive compulsive behaviour. It ruined some people's marriages. Luckily I wasn't married, and now I understand why I'm not!*

JB: The book takes a very scientific and environmentally active stance throughout, which was and is unusual in a fishing book. Can you explain why this was so?

RG: *It is partly because I started off as a fish biologist, I have a professional background there. The publishers did request that the book be interesting to anglers, interesting to anglers of a scientific mind, and also of value to first-year college and university students. So, it had something of an academic content. Also, I think scientists have failed to give the scientific information to anglers that they deserve, and I wanted to provide some of the more technical information. It takes a bit of digesting but the reader can hopefully have something more than a sporting ethos and can appreciate the importance of the quarry and its broader significance.*

JB: How has knowledge of ferox trout and charr moved forward since the publication of the book?

RG: *Most of the book remains viable, from a scientific point of view, but we have moved on. For example, we used to wonder whether ferox were an ambush predator with a very narrow defined territory from which they ambushed their prey, or whether they hunted more like cheetahs, ranging about. Well, the truth is a bit more intermediate. Ferox have a 'home range', but it is quite a big one. They'll move 6 miles up a loch. At Loch Garry they will move from one end to the other; this is what Alistair Thorne found out. And they will also use a wide depth range, so we now know more about how the ferox rove around. But, we also know that when they are recaptured it is usually on the shore where they were first caught. We have more information on DNA now, particularly with the charr, increasing the perspective of the diversity of Arctic charr. It is incredible what we have … it is going to tell us so much more about how the whole environment evolved after the ice melted.*

JB: I read your paper on Rannoch recently …

RG: *Well there are three kinds of charr on Rannoch. We still argue about whether they are fully specific or not but they are certainly separate genetic populations. It is Galapagos finches under the water, that's how important it is. We now have a great deal of evidence to suggest there were two main colonisation groups/routes … Scotland has one group of charr that are related to the Baltic, Scandinavian and Western Russian charr and another group that we share with the Irish, and there are variations within these. Amazing stuff! It rams home that the ferox and the charr are really a living inheritance from the Ice Age. The Ice Age underwater hasn't gone away. We are still dealing with a pro-glacial environment that is phenomenal. It gives an understanding of all the other animals, some of which are missing now – I like to think that we could definitely have had our own endemic population of reindeer at one time. And lynx, distinct from the European ones as well. Even the grouse. It is all part of how Scotland was isolated and then recolonised. The ferox and the charr stimulate so much interest in the total environment.*

JB: You grew up in Glasgow, catching sticklebacks and small trout …

RG: *I was lucky to have a father who took me up to catch sticklebacks in the local pond. And then I got a bit bigger and he took me up to Loch Lomond and the Trossochs lochs and Rannoch Moor, and so he interested me in fish. And Glasgow's a handy place, you can get out of it and in forty minutes you're in a rural area; 10 miles from the city centre you can catch wild brown trout. So although I lived in an industrial environment, I was lucky to have the rural one next door.*

JB: So why ferox trout?

RG: *I was always fascinated with predators, with big fish, and when my dad took me up to the fishing tackle shops in Glasgow, there were ferox there in big cases and I heard the guys talking about who had caught them, and some of them were still catching them. So I just got this wee boy's fascination with big fish, like wee boys do … like they do with dinosaurs or sharks. For me it was ferox. Later on, I became a freshwater biologist and took a job at the fish lab at Pitlochry, and I noticed while I was there that among the literature there wasn't much done on the Scottish charr and so I just started. I realised in fact that almost nothing had been done, so I have been very, very privileged to pioneer that branch of research in Scotland, with others.*

JB: Your book mentions the Ferox 85 group. Are they still going?

RG: *The Ferox 85 group are still there, Aya Thorne and his brother, the Special Relentless Squadron, they are still there. I'm nearly 60, some of us are in our seventies, but we are still out there. The ferox don't know we're old gits!*

JB: I also read your paper on non-indigenous fish introductions to the Spey lochs, how real are the dangers?

RG: *The dangers are very real, some of them are latent but they are still there. What is difficult to get across, even to senior members of SNH, is the timeline – these issues can lie dormant for thirty years and suddenly explode. The analogy is there with rabbits. Rabbits in Britain were struggling for centuries until there was a change in the landscape with the agricultural revolution, and suddenly, whoosh, they're off … it can be at a low level and then you can have a population explosion and your native stocks are threatened. Now, the big danger to the ecology of charr in Scottish lochs is the roach, and the introduction of non-native pike to places where they should not have been. It is better now that pike anglers are behaving more responsibly, but I know in the past there was quite a lot of moving of pike when there should not have been, and then the next stage is the live bait. Luckily we have now got a live bait ban, but when you have got people going to reservoirs with colostomy bags with live fish in them … that is what you're up against. There are pike anglers that actually did that.*

JB: What other threats exist more broadly to the ecology of the Highlands?

RG: *Global warming, if it exists, could be a problem. We've noticed that if there is a warm autumn then the recruitment of charr is not so good in the following year. Charr need cold water. But, we have no idea of long-term cyclicity; we know in the Middle Ages it was warmer than it is now and charr still survived; we may have lost charr in lochs we don't know, but the problem now is that we have warming at a time when people are moving non-native fish about – that didn't happen before, so now we have got the double indemnity and very often it's a combination of factors. Charr are very good at surviving in difficult places but they are not highly competitive fish. In a vestigial area like this they may be threatened by species better adapted to warmer conditions.*

JB: We spoke recently about ferox changing their feeding habits to predate on coarse fish, for example on Windermere and Corrib. I'm no scientist but this worries me. Where can you see this going?

RG: *So far so good, but Humpty Dumpty could shout that when he was falling to the ground. Humpty Dumpty was fine all the way down until he went splat. We might be in the Humpty Dumpty scenario now. Predators do frequently switch to the main fish supply because it is an easier source and they might do that. But in North America, for example, the native predators have not switched to eating the European ruffe the way they have in Loch Lomond, so you've no guarantee. We don't know what will happen in fifty years. It might be good in the short term, but in the long term we don't know. We tend to think in given life spans – the only people who have anywhere near the understanding of this kind of thinking are foresters. We have to think with a forester's mentality, with a long-term approach.*

JB: When I caught my first ferox your book had been out for a year or two, and nobody I fished with knew anything about them. Now there are DVDs available and ferox captures on YouTube. Your thoughts?

RG: *I'm happy. One of the points of the book was to make people realise that ferox fishing was part of this great cultural experience of the Highlands – as much as stags, deer, that kind of thing. It was an iconic species, still is to me, and it was part of an angling culture and a societal culture as well. The main defence against something going missing is having a group of people who are interested in it. Now we have a whole group of people who realise the importance of ferox, even at the simple level of wanting to catch one. They realise it is important, they realise it is special, and I am happy that we have helped ferox fishing back out of obscurity. I'm glad that people are following the catch-and-release policy now. I never used to believe in it myself until Alistair Thorne showed me it was possible for these fish to be hooked several times and released, on quite brutal tackle, and to grow and do very well. I'm happy with the ferox cult and hopefully it will increase the pressure on the politicians to manage them because we have a world-class resource. The ferox trout fishing in Scotland is some of the best on the planet. The only way to look after that is to look after the environment that produces it. You have to have a total system management plan to manage the ferox.*

JB: Over thirty years ago you hitched around the Highlands planting indigenous trees to protect this environment. What would you suggest a young ferox tyro should do now, in 2010?

RG: *I would say get involved in some kind of conservation group. They didn't exist when I did it. That was in 1974. What we have now is a kind of conservation ethos. I would say don't vanish up your left nostril about it, the Highlands is a cultural environment as much as a natural one, so take your part in that culture but certainly support reforesting with native trees, get out there and take part in rehabilitating. I've often said, 'the Highlands are not a wasteland ripe for development, they are a wasted land ready for rehabilitation', so go out there and help to rehabilitate it.*

JB: Finally, for those of us who find catching ferox an exercise in relentlessness and unanswered prayers, can you suggest one tip that isn't in the book?

RG: *Don't get too worried about what lure or what bait you've got on, just get out there and do it. Any big lure or reasonably sized bait will do; the main ingredient is still sheer relentless effort. Even people who have caught records, several times over, have long, empty blank days nonetheless. Just apply yourself – most of the tricks of how to go about it are still true, but don't get hung up on the magic bullet approach. There isn't one!*

Ron's time was up; the charr of an unnamed loch were awaiting his attentions. There was so much I had wanted to talk about – the legacy of Colquhoun and the Victorian tyros, the possibility of a new book encompassing more up-to-date scientific work, the Ferox 85 group's recent adventures on Lochs Kildermorie and Glass – but it would all have to wait for another day. There was just time for the author to sign my tatty copy of *Ferox Trout and Arctic Charr*. The inscription said:

> To Jon – with the compliments of the author – and may all your ferox be just slightly smaller than mine! Ron Greer

And then he was gone, striding off towards the hills and the lochs, and another project.

Five hundred miles and more lay ahead of Vic and me that day, but there was no need to hurry. I wandered through the restaurant and took a final look at the giant salmon on each wall. The thought of native brown trout reaching such a size seemed preposterous, but the men of Perthshire were getting closer every day to proving otherwise. One day, it would happen. Before I left the restaurant for the long road south I made a silent wish – when Scotland's first 40lb ferox is hooked, the man on the other end of the line should be the guru.

25

UISGE BEATHA – THE WATER OF LIFE

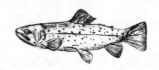

I was 7 years old when I first went to Bodle's Burn. The stream was vibrant; it flowed strongly with depth and vigour. It was full of small trout, too, and Ricky showed my brother and me how we could tempt them from the water with worms and a hook. It was the first magic that Chris and I had ever witnessed first-hand, and nothing since has compared to it. As we marched back to our grandmother's house at the end of that day, I told my cousin and my brother that fishing was the best thing ever – better than *Doctor Who* and curly wurlies, better even than Action Man – and I would do it for the rest of my life. My two companions agreed and made similar declarations. We all kept that promise.

Bodle's Burn ran out of the graveyard where our grandmother and her sister would one day be buried, under the old main road and through some woods, and ended at a pool in the grounds of a house. This small, 1-acre water was known to local boys as The Dam. There was a fence around it but it was only waist height, and the occupants of the house turned a blind eye to the bubble floats and worms that were flung over this fence towards the fish. The bigger ones lived here, genuine ¾-pounders, and my second trout was one of them. I was 8 then, but can still remember the taste of its white flesh, grilled with butter by my grandmother and served up with coarse brown bread on the back porch of her house in Munro Terrace.

I was 41 when I returned to Bodle's Burn. Chris, Edward and Vic were with me and shared the deflation I felt when I saw it. Time had not been overly kind to me, but for the burn it had been calamitous. All flow had gone. The water above the main road was a still, stagnant artery on the southern edge of a housing estate and little moved below its surface. On its muddy bottom were beer cans, bicycle wheels, discarded children's toys and all manner of detritus from a world that cared little for small streams or the memories of middle-aged men. We crossed the road and looked for The Dam, but found only an industrial estate. All landmarks had disappeared, and if The Dam was still there, we couldn't find it. It was a perfect tragedy.

That day, and the subsequent meeting with Ron, got me thinking about trout in the Highlands and about the broader needs of the Highland environment. As we drove south, I told Vic that the Scotland I had come to know during the ferox hunt, the Highlands that Ricky had led my brother and me to as children, was in peril. I didn't know the extent of the threat but I knew it was there. Bodle's Burn had confirmed it.

To survive and prosper, trout need clean, oxygenated water and a supply of food. They need cover and sunlight and a few other things besides, but without good water and food, they are done for. Most species of fish are the same, but trout are fussier than the majority; muddy puddles won't do – unless you're a corpulent bath-reared rainbow with low expectations – and warm waters with low oxygen levels can be a graveyard. The juvenile brownies in the burn wouldn't have stood a chance.

I remember reading a book when I was a boy which was called something like *Through the Fish's Eye*. Though the exact title has been lost to me over time, its scientific consideration of the fish we wanted to catch was memorable. It was written by a couple of

Americans so there was mention of muskies and brook trout and walleyes, but they remembered the ordinary fish too, the ones my brother and I went looking for after school and at weekends, and they told us what their lives were like. My brother and I learnt from the book that fish would behave differently according to the weather, wind and other circumstances. It wouldn't always be as simple as throwing a worm under the bridge of a burn.

The book said that temperature was the most important factor in governing fish behaviour and survival. I remembered that bit clearly, and everything I have learnt as an angler since then has seemed to support it. But temperature is not the whole story. A drop in the level of oxygen, even by such an apparently tiny fraction as two parts per million, can be fatal.

Chris and I learnt this first-hand, and we were about 10 years old when it happened. We had been taken by our ever-patient mother to fish a small pool in the grounds of a pub in Lee-on-Solent. It was a Saturday afternoon in late summer and we had played football that morning. Our team, the Highlands Colts, had beaten Collingwood Under-11s by fourteen goals to nil. I had scored twice. My brother, who was a defender and under strict instructions never to cross the halfway line, had even managed to bag a goal of his own. It had been a rout, but was nothing compared to what we experienced that afternoon.

We had maggots and bread and were float-fishing for perch and whatever else came along, but there was a group of boys next to us fishing for carp. They were serious fisher-boys; they smoked and swore with confidence and had camouflaged jackets, and we were told by our mother to stay away from them. They were casting big crusts of bread under a tree and, at the hottest point of the afternoon, a pair of lips sucked their bread down. This led to much activity and Chris and I reeled in our own rods to watch. One of the boys took on the fish while his friends offered advice and crouched ready with a large net. The fish was obviously big ('fuckin' massive' according to the boy holding the rod), and the drama took some time to reach its conclusion. When it did, even mother was curious enough to suggest we go and have a look. 'Try to ignore their language,' she said.

The carp was a fat mirror and weighed 14lb, and we joined the crowd that crouched around it in disbelief. The victorious boy lost his seriousness and grinned broadly as photographs were taken. Backs were patted, and with great ceremony the carp was returned. We watched in silence as it waddled across the shallow swim and back to the shade of its tree.

My brother and I decided we would have to return and try for one. Dad was due back from sea in a few weeks and he would take us. It was arranged with precision, resolve and determination. He would collect us from school on a Thursday and take us to the giant carp of The Inn by the Sea. We would go for an evening, fishing into dark when we would have the pool to ourselves. We had three weeks to wait, and they were the slowest three weeks of our young lives.

It was dusk when we arrived, and though the light was going, we could see that something was wrong. The pool had almost vanished. In every pitch the water was only inches deep, and in some places it had gone altogether. There was a strange, malevolent smell hanging over the pool. Dad marched us into the pub to find out what had gone wrong.

The publican told us a sorry tale. The lake had all but dried up since our last visit, a breach in the dam had seen to that, and the hot weather had added to the misery. Dad asked whether there were any carp left to fish for. 'No chance,' said the publican. 'The water had no oxygen left in it and they all died within a couple of days. Gasping, they were. Now, can I get the three of you some drinks while you're here?'

So we knew all about the calamities that could befall small waters when temperatures rose or oxygen levels fell. The little pool recovered and we fished there as teenagers, but we were always aware that its survival was precariously balanced.

I always thought differently about Scotland. The cooler climate and huge volume of water in the Highlands offer an unscientific reassurance that all is well. But the vastness of the landscape instils a confidence that may be misplaced. The rivers and lochs of the Highlands are as fragile, in their own way, as a sun-baked carp pool in Lee-on-Solent. A 1995 investigation by the Scottish government into water quality in Scottish lochs revealed that 30 of the 200 lochs sampled showed evidence of depleted water quality. Acidification, agriculture, sewage, forestry, fish farming and urban drainage all featured among the causes, but the research was deliberately narrow in its focus. No account was taken of the ecological effects of non-indigenous fish introductions, or of subsequent changes to the food chain. The decline of charr and the ascendancy of roach, rudd, ruffe, pike and rainbow trout are less apparent to the casual observer, but are as disastrous in their own way as any of the other threats. The battle is not only one of preserving water and land quality, but of protecting the post-glacial integrity of the Highlands. Thankfully, men like Greer are on the case, but they cannot do it alone.

Ferox trout are a small part of the picture, but they are at least now in the frame. The Ferox 85 group and the anglers who have followed their lead have demystified a fish that was almost forgotten. Ferox were dinosaurs, monsters even, when Ricky and the boys and I began looking for them. Our perspective was naive but unsurprising, given the paucity of contemporary information and the mystique attached to them by old literature. This is no longer so. Ferox live in many Scottish lochs, in all probability in greater numbers than we realise, and do so successfully – just as they have since the ice retreated thousands of years ago. Old angling prejudices that dismissed trolling as mindless piscatorial thuggery have waned, and now even the fly-fishing press publish occasional ferox pieces as an antidote to the 'five flies I wouldn't leave home without' articles. Anglers, editors and conservationists are agreed on one critical fact: ferox, alongside the smaller indigenous species, are an indicator of good, healthy fishing water and of the survival of a landscape that only we, as humans, are in a position to destroy.

In short, ferox belong in the lochs of Perthshire and Sutherland, just as they do in the big lakes of Wales and the Lake District, and the limestone expanses of Ireland, and their presence is to be celebrated. It ought also to be protected.

The Scotland which stole my heart in the 1990s is changing. The Beauly-Denny Landscape Group, the Ramblers' Association, the Scottish Wild Land Group and others have had to take up the fight recently against power lines and wind factories, and against inevitable change brought by increased population and new industry. In an age of enforced austerity, they have the difficult job of persuading Holyrood that the cheapest option is not always the best option for Scotland. Much has been made of the sea-to-sea glory of the Highlands and the need to protect its landscape, but its defendants know that this is more than a question of aesthetics, of Luddite resistance to modern encroachments or the protection of a Scotland that might, in the near future, exist only in memory. The fundamental attraction of the Highlands, the essence that draws in the tourists and the fishermen, is the post-glacial landscape and its waters. Scotland, like anywhere, must grow and adapt to survive, but it must do so in a way that protects the very things that make it unique.

I went to Scotland to see Ricky and rediscover the Fraser half of my family, to catch fish and breathe in good, clean air. I went to reclaim a childhood that had been idyllic and thrilling in equal measure, and in ferox I found a reason to keep returning. Thirteen years have passed since the adventure began. The black waters of Shin have not changed. The brooding depths of Veyatie are as unspoilt as ever. Kildermorie, but for the wind farm that overlooks it, is as wild now as it was when I cast there as a boy. Fishing stills means more to me than curly wurlies, *Doctor Who* and Action Man. It is still the thing I want to do for the rest of my life – but Bodle's Burn is gone, and though it was only ever an insignificant stream in a country that has thousands of them, it was special because it was alive. Beautiful wild trout were once there, and in the clear cool water of the Scottish Highlands it should always be so.

26

WADE IN THE WATER

When I was a boy, standing on the shores of Kildermorie with Ricky and Chris, there was a secret part of me that wanted to run, to get to the end of the last road and keep going until there was nothing left but me, the sky and the mountains. In my young mind, I could forage and fish, dodge school forever and become a caveman with a long beard and no responsibilities. Ricky and Chris would have been welcome to join me but I was smart enough not to ask them. I knew that they would give me a strange sideways look and say, 'yeah, good idea', and return to their fishing thinking that their companion had been out in the sun too long. It wasn't a normal way for a boy to think, but I thought it all the same.

This temptation to run has never been far from the surface and has occasionally returned – never more so than during the years I spent in Sutherland. Every time I drove north I was abandoning a life, albeit temporarily, that was hard to make sense of; I couldn't change it and I couldn't live with it, but I could come to terms with it when sat in a boat with Ricky. None of it mattered when I was there.

The feeling came back in Ireland. The quiet life of Oughterard, with its green hills, cosy pubs and lough full of giant trout, had Vic and I asking the same question – why should we ever go home? We could do without our jobs, our house, our bills and responsibilities. We wouldn't miss them at all. If our cat, Pumpkin, had been with us, we may never have returned to England again. But, of course, the feeling subsided and we crossed the Irish Sea, and within days were back in our respective classrooms, with only photographs to remind us of what we had left behind.

When I was very young and became a fisherman, I had no burdens from which to escape. School was fun. Girls were pretty and interesting to look at, but irrelevant. Money was meaningless. There were no wars to steal my father away. But I still felt a desire to escape the confines of the playground and be among the woods and the streams and to get my hands dirty.

My brother and I grew up in an age when boys were expected to be out of the house between dawn and dusk; scrabbling around forbidden ponds and streams was considered only a minor form of delinquency. This was the late seventies and so the adults in our lives were just relieved that we weren't sniffing glue.

Nobody ever told us that we should grow out of it, either – and so we didn't. Back then, fishing felt like a necessary ingredient in a good life, and now, almost forty years on, it still does. But we live in a century of psycho-babble and self-help groups, and compulsive behaviours come with labels. Now, obsessions must be analysed.

Most of the men that I know take their fishing rather seriously. That's not to say that they can't live, work and function within society's more usual parameters, but it is done with a grudging acceptance. They will do just as much as is required to earn their money, but with a silent defiance they will think about roach, trout or carp while they do it.

For other men – and it *is* usually men – it may be golf or football, but it is always something. We really do seem unable to stop ourselves. Are we sating a now-redundant hunting instinct? Reclaiming our masculinity in these gender-aware times? Are we finding ways to avoid the pressures and expectations of a grown-up life, if only for a while? Or are we just selfish, chest-beating bastards who are closer to our Neanderthal brothers than we would like to admit?

I don't know, and I am not sure I would like to, either. I do know, though, that fishing feels beautiful and poetic, vital and life-affirming, and if serious types wish to discuss my reasons for doing it, they can find me down by the river.

Ferox trout did become an obsession, intensely so for three years and to a lesser extent ever since. They offered a narrative thread to a life that was otherwise aimless. They were wild and fascinating, and so my behaviour could be easily defended against those who thought I ought to be settling down and behaving more conventionally. A fisherman's greatest prizes are his memories, and in the waters of Sutherland and Easter Ross, Ricky and I gathered our share. Above all, the search for *salmo ferox* was just so much fun. Looking back, I am unrepentant.

I went fishing yesterday. Vic came with me, and we spent the day on a Suffolk broad, chasing pike. The fishing was simple, almost lazy, casting deadbaits and float tackle from a hired boat. I caught three pike between 6 and 21lb, and I caught them easily. There was no dazzling skill involved, just a willingness to get out there and do it and to be ready when something happened. I used the old Hardy spinning rods that Simon sold to me in 1998 and, fifty years after their manufacture, they were as reliable as ever.

Throughout the day the air got colder and the sky clearer, and it was all too evident that the seasons had changed once more. It was pike weather. We got back to Wiltshire at midnight and found a thin layer of frost waiting for us, and this morning I brought in some logs and lit the first fire of the new winter.

For the next few months I shall fish for pike, grayling and perch. All three species are indigenous to the waters around me and are plentiful. Perch, especially, are experiencing a renaissance and are being caught to great sizes from the local rivers. Grayling can be found in the shallower runs and they will give me an excuse to put on waders and walk waist-deep into each pool with my fly rod. The water will be cold, deliciously so, and the air will freeze in front of my face with every breath. I shall think about ferox trout, of course, but I won't fish for them until spring arrives and the urge to drive north, or west, becomes too strong to ignore.

Perhaps it is because I am getting older, but my fishing doesn't always have to be an adventure, a road trip to a new world. Usually it is not. A few stolen hours by the Bristol Avon with a rod, bag and net will often suffice, and I am home before supper. Brief moments wandering its upper reaches, among its farmland and copses, are enough to satisfy an urge that has been there for a long, long time. And if, while I am out, my float disappears and I find life on the end of my line, I will be taken momentarily back to a small Scottish burn, with Chris and Ricky by my side. For a few seconds, I will have escaped.

After all, in the wilderness and by the water, we are all children.